Start a Commercial or Residential Cleaning Business

By Robert Donaldson

ISBN-13: 978-1496113924

ISBN-10: 1496113926

Published in the United States of America

Foreword

This book is but one in a series of publications aimed at helping others learn how to start a small, independently run business. As the saying goes, "Give a man a fish and you feed him for a day. Teach a man to fish and he feeds himself for a lifetime." It is my hope that by writing this book, I will teach someone how to think and to work like an independent businessperson.

Before there were factories and assembly lines and huge multinational corporations, there was the family with its small spot of land from which the family drew it sustenance. The landowner worked the land and grew crops and raised livestock and poultry which he sold to neighbors and nearby townspeople. Mother, father and children were all involved with the task of providing for the family. This was the original spirit of America—the spirit of freedom and independence.

Somewhere along the way that spirit of freedom and independence somehow got lost in the shuffle. The Industrial Revolution ushered in an age of dependence and reliance on the process of working for someone else in order to feed one's family. Later there came the spirit of depending on the federal and state governments to act as a "safety net" to help families in dire straits.

The citizens of the world must change their thinking and change it quickly. At the time I started writing this book in January, 2014, the unemployment rate for the United States of America was hovering around 7%. I looked at this figure and thought, *There is something wrong here.* I realized that we as Americans and the citizens of other nations had surrendered our freedom and independence in return for the dependence on others for our own financial security.

Childhood obesity has risen at an alarming rate of the last three decades. Type 2 diabetes now threatens the health of generations to come. Our children spend more time at the computer than they spend exercising. Nobody wants to work anymore. Nobody wants to exert him- or herself in performing any physical activity.

That is not to say that the entire population lives sedentary lives. There are millions of workers who perform jobs that are physically demanding. There are those among us whose jobs require them to clean the homes and offices of doctors and lawyers and many other professionals. Why not take it a step further and start your own business of offering cleaning services to others.

There is no shame in working in the cleaning industry any more so than there is in working in a factory. The real difference is that by owning your own janitorial or cleaning business, you can earn considerably more money than you would by working for someone else. This brings us to the heart of the matter.

You might be paid seven to ten dollars an hour for cleaning someone else's home or business. With you own cleaning service business you can make upwards of fifty dollars an hour. Of course there are expenses involved with running your own business. You simply charge a price that allows for expenses and a tidy profit to boot.

Many are tired of living under the cloud of uncertainty, wondering when the axe will fall and they get their lay-off notice. There are those forward thinking persons who are thinking of starting a small business but don't know where to find information and details on doing so. That is the purpose and intent of this book—to offer guidance to those who do want to break away from the nine to five treadmill of living from paycheck to paycheck. This book was written for the independent thinkers. This book was written for you.

I started with the aim of providing as much detailed information as I could about starting and running a cleaning service business. Let's not kid ourselves here. You will have to do further research to work out the details of running your own business. I have not gone into minute detail about operating your business. This is more of a broad overview aimed at inspiring you to look further and to dig deeper into the industry and learn as much as you can, gaining the confidence that you want and need to start your own janitorial or cleaning service business. This is just the first step in the ongoing process of starting your own business. There are many intermediate steps that need to be taken as you continue to learn and to grow in knowledge and confidence.

I hope that this book reaches the audience for whom it was intended. I hope that you become inspired and motivated and excited as you read. That in itself has been my humble intent from the beginning.

While this book is arranged in chapters that contain many details on starting and operating your janitorial or cleaning service business, it is not by any means all-inclusive. At times, it might seem rather repetitive. This is by design because many will read this book from cover-to- cover while others will use it as a reference, focusing on particular areas that interest them. I suggest that you read the entire book chapter by chapter at least once. Then refer to specific chapter as the need arises.

Table of Contents

Chapter 1

Introduction

The purpose of this book is to provide timely information for the startup and operation of a small one to two person cleaning operation with a team made up of a husband and wife. This book is also ideal to start your cleaning business as a family operation with parents and children or relatives all working together to generate income. There is special benefit in starting small to learn the business. If you wish, you can later expand your business to include more services and take on employees from outside the business. That's the beauty of starting a cleaning business –you can become as large as you want or stay small and cultivate a short list of clients, focusing on providing the highest quality service.

You will often see the terms "cleaning business," "cleaning service" and "janitorial service" used interchangeable here. These terms all refer to cleaning properties owned, rented or leased by a business to perform some service or sales operation.

One of your greatest challenges in starting your cleaning business is in getting past the image of this being menial work. As a business owner you will work for much more than minimum wage. You are the head manager and chief operations officer. As such, you will make important decisions on scheduling, ordering supplies and running the company.

A cleaning business involves hard work, a commitment to excellence and dedication. Your business can become a source of great pride for you and your family and it will offer the reward of being your own boss and making as much as you want by working more.

Cleaning services, including both commercial and residential cleaning and maintenance is projected to be one of the fastest growing businesses for 2014. Growth in real estate occupancy is one of the major forces driving the demand for janitorial and cleaning services. The cleaning industry is one of the fastest growing industries in the world. As the owner of a cleaning business, you can make you cleaning business as broadly or narrowly focused as you choose. You might want to take on a few office cleaning jobs in your local area. You might want to specialize in cleaning only small business offices like those of doctors, lawyers, real estate agents and the like. Another option could be to focus only on cleaning the display windows for stores and shops. The residential cleaning area is a rapidly growing area of expertise since there are now many families in which both husband and wife have full time jobs. Having someone else do the job is a winning situation for the families and for your business.

The workers involved in cleaning businesses perform many duties. They sweep, mop, dust furniture, clean windows, clean restrooms and bathrooms, vacuum carpets, shampoo carpets, clean drapes and many other duties. While working in the cleaning business is not as physically demanding as working in some factories, it will sometime be necessary to lift and move moderately heavy items like vacuum cleaners and buffing machines. One of the major advantages of having a cleaning business is that offers repeat business. Things have to be cleaned again and again whether in commercial or residential properties.

According to the Small Business Development Center Network, the cleaning services industry is expected to expand rapidly and revenue is forecast to increase 3.3% per year to total $47.7 billion by 2016. These projections clearly indicate that now is a great time to start a cleaning business.

Starting a small cleaning business requires little capital outlay and the startup costs are usually less than $2,000. An office cleaning business is an excellent opportunity that you can start while keeping your current job and, as business grows, and you gain more contracts and earn more income, you can expand into a larger operation, hiring others to sell and provide cleaning services within your city or county. The first year potential income for an office cleaning business is about $40,000. The typical pricing you might charge for cleaning a 5,000 square foot office might be between $40 and $100 per cleaning.

You should be able to clean an office this size in about an hour. If you have 40 office cleaning jobs per month –cleaning two offices each night and charging $39.95 per cleaning, then you will earn $1600 per month for about 40 man-hours of work for the month. There are few other part-time jobs out there that pay as well, and the fact that you are working for yourself makes it even better.

Remember that your supplies and expenses will be paid from this $1600 per month. To make more money, just get more clients and do more work. A two member husband/wife team can easily handle 80 man-hours per month and make over $3,000 per month gross income. Start small with your office cleaning business with your eye to the future and growing and expanding your business.

Further growth is tied to expansion of services and adding new clients. During the first few years of operation, you would most likely seek out prospective clients yourself. However, it is recommended that the owner should soon hire a salesperson to acquire contracts while he or she focuses on ensuring the quality of services provided.

One thing to keep in mind is that the cleaning services industry is tied to the real estate market. The recession of 2009 led to a decrease in commercial property rentals and sales. Consequently, the cleaning services industry also lost ground. Know your industry thoroughly and subscribe to financial publications such as the Wall Street Journal, Forbes and Barron's. It is important that you, as a business owner, keep your finger, so to speak, on the pulse of the economy. Downturns in the economy can be anticipated and adjustments to your business plan can be made, allowing you to weather any economic storm. While your cleaning services business can experience an occasional economic hiccup, it is your responsibility as the owner to plan for every contingency so that your business can grow and thrive through all economic conditions. Keep in mind that your cleaning service business is the lifeline that provides for the needs and wants of your family. It is important early on that you take your business seriously and do all that you can to ensure its success.

A home-based cleaning business allows for flexibility in scheduling. You can choose the hours you want to work, keeping in mind that most clients will want their businesses cleaned after business hours –usually after 5PM during the week, and on weekends. You and your employees will often be entrusted with keys to the premises. Any losses or damages sustained as a result of the actions of your employees reflect upon your company itself. As your business grows and you start to take on employees, make sure that you hire only trustworthy people since the future of your success is directly tied to you and your workers. The level of your success in this business grows in direct proportion to your performance and your reputation.

Many new companies have found that it is more practical and financially advantageous to contract out commercial cleaning services than to have in-house cleaners. Companies can save on benefits like health insurance and other costs by hiring and independent cleaning contractor. The independent cleaning contractor provides a needed service and creates much needed jobs.

Before you consider starting a cleaning service business, you must decide whether this business is right for you. Cleaning offices and homes for other people is different from cleaning your own home. You might have to clean several properties during your shift. Cleaning is physically demanding work. Make sure you are in good physical condition. Your work will involve quite a bit of standing, bending, reaching, kneeling and other repetitive activity.

It is important to have good organizational skills to run your cleaning business. Matters such as taxes, ordering supplies and scheduling jobs require that you be able to use your time wisely.

You will need good customer relations skills in the operation of your cleaning business. You and your employees will communicate regularly with clients. Always be courteous. Listen closely to any concerns expressed and assure the client that any problems will be taken care of quickly.

Have a reserve of at least six months savings when you start your cleaning business. You never know when something might come up where you have to buy some unexpected supplies or equipment at the spur of the moment.

Make sure that your transportation is reliable. You can use your personal vehicle at first. Be sure to get business insurance added to you auto insurance policy as soon as you get your first contract. Keep your vehicle well maintained and serviced. You don't want to have to reschedule a cleaning appointment because your truck broke down. You need to think ahead to avoid delays and disruptions.

Your clothing should always be neat and clean. If you can't afford uniforms in the beginning, you can have t-shirts printed with you company name and logo. This goes a long way in cultivating a professional image.

5 Reasons to Start Your Own Cleaning Service Business

Many people feel that the only way to have financial freedom and independence is by working for someone else. On the contrary, working for yourself in your own cleaning service business provides a higher level of financial security. The independent thinking entrepreneur knows that financial security can only be realized when they themselves are in charge of their finances.

Many people are fearful and insecure about looking out for themselves. You must motivate yourself to take the reins of your life and make your own choices and decisions that will make your dreams of financial security and independence into reality.

The job of cleaning other people's homes or offices might, on the surface, seem like drudgery. But when you see start your business grow and see that the large amounts of money coming in, this will quickly change your thinking about cleaning.

I'd like to list here some of the many reasons to start your own cleaning service business.

1. **You Are Your Own Boss.** As the owner of your own cleaning service business, you get to "call the shots." You make the decisions and therefore it is you who determines how much money you will earn.

2. **Unlimited Earnings Potential.** You can grow and expand your cleaning business as much or as little as you choose. You can stay small with a few clients that you service in your spare time while keeping your full-time job. You can also expand your business to include specialty services such as carpet cleaning, window cleaning and move in/out home and apartment cleaning. You will quickly realize that there is no limit to how much can grow your cleaning business.

3. **Low Startup Cost.** You can start your cleaning service business for anything from a few hundred dollars to a few thousand dollars. You don't need a huge outlay of capital to get started. You probably already have enough money saved to get your business up and running within a couple of weeks.

4. **You Choose Your Hours of Work.** As a small business owner, you get to set your own hours and work part-time to start.
5. **Get Paid Every Day.** Once you get you cleaning service business up and running, you will create a regular flow of cash that seem endless. It's not unusual to get a check for your services every day you work.

Chapter 2

Types of Cleaning Service Businesses

A cleaning service business is a business whose function and major operations are devoted to cleaning either commercial or residential properties or both. Cleaning service businesses can be divided into two major categories that span the industry. **Commercial cleaning** businesses are concerned with cleaning stores, offices, warehouses, factories and similar commercial business operations. **Residential cleaning** businesses focus on cleaning residential properties for homeowners and renters. A growing field of residential cleaning is in providing clean-up after residents move out and before new residents move in. Also included in this category is the need for cleaning the exterior surfaces of mobile and motor homes.

Many cleaning service businesses later expand into other specialized areas of cleaning including:

- Window cleaning service
- Carpet and floor cleaning service
- Residential maid service
- Drapery cleaning service
- Live plants care
- Pressure cleaning

As you grow your business, consider expanding your service into these areas. Doing so will increase your customer base and income. Always keep an eye to the future. Cultivate a professional attitude within yourself and your employees.

As you can see, the cleaning services industry offers many opportunities for the small and independent business owner to earn income. Start-up costs are low and initial outlay is reasonable. Starting out, try to focus on offering commercial cleaning for small offices and stores in your area. Later, as you gain confidence in your ability to do an excellent job, consider taking on larger office buildings and complexes. Many of your larger clients will provide their own equipment and supplies such as mops, buckets, buffers, brooms and cleaning chemicals. You, as the cleaning services provider, will only need to go to the business and perform the necessary cleaning duties.

Residential and commercial cleaning involves different processes, depending, of course, on what the client wants cleaned. Some of your smaller office cleaning jobs might take an hour or two to complete. Larger jobs might take several hours and require that two or more team members work together.

Starting out, you should give your cost estimate based on what needs to be cleaned and how long it will take. Be sure to charge enough to make it worth your while to do the job. Also take into consideration the fact that you need to charge enough so that you can buy more equipment and supplies to take on bigger jobs. Eventually, you will need to hire someone to help.

We will get into more detail about estimating, bidding, customer care, cleaning procedures and other matters later.

Chapter 3

Getting Started

There are certain equipment and supplies that you will to need to get and keep on hand for you cleaning service business. The list below, though not all inclusive, is a basic inventory that any cleaning business should replenish as needed.

- Vacuum cleaner
- Heavy duty extension cords for vacuum
- Broom
- Dust pan
- White cloth towels
- Paper towels
- Wet mop and bucket
- Dry mop
- Latex gloves
- Dust masks
- "Wet Floor" Warning signs
- Feather dusters
- Long handle duster
- Toilet brush
- Toilet bowl cleaner
- Disinfectant cleaner
- Soft scrub cleaner for fiberglass sinks
- General purpose bathroom cleaner
- Window cleaner
- Furniture polish
- Plastic and steel wool scrubbing pads
- Large sponges

- Caddy for carrying cleaning supplies

Most of these items can be purchased from your local hardware and home supply store. Keep in mind that much of your equipment and supplies are business expense items and therefore deductible to a certain extent. Keep track of the receipts for all your purchases. You might need to employ the services of a good bookkeeper or learn to keep your own records. Remember that whatever you need to know about starting and running a cleaning business can be found online. You just have to search for the information.

Preparing Yourself Mentally for the Task Ahead

Many people start small businesses each year and many fail miserably. The main reason for failure is uncertainty. Many go into business with doubts that they will succeed. They set up obstacles for themselves even before they start. As a businessperson, you must first of all believe in yourself. You might not know everything about the cleaning business starting out, but you must keep an open mind and be willing to learn.

Henry Ford once said, "If you think you can do a thing or think you can't do a thing, you're right."

Recognize this truth. Write it down and post it someplace where you can read it every day. Put it on your bulletin board. Place it beside your computer. Place it in your wallet and read it and tell yourself this fact every day.

There will certainly be obstacles that arise in the course of perfecting the operations of your business. You can do this! It is not brain surgery. It has been done before and it can and will be done again. Starting any business requires stead effort. Focus your thoughts each day on learning more details about the cleaning industry and you will succeed. Always move forward and you will succeed.

There will be those who will be jealous of your efforts to enjoy financial freedom and independence. There will always be naysayers who will try to discourage you. There will always be those who do not have the self-motivation and determination to launch their own business and are eager to discourage anyone who tries to escape to financial freedom. Do not let these people discourage you. Use them as motivation to work even harder to succeed in your own cleaning service business.

Always forward! Always upward! Make this your motto.

There are certain people whose advice you should avoid when starting your cleaning service business. They are:

The know-it-all. These are the people who might have lots of theories about how to run a cleaning service business. They might even have tried and failed at running a similar business. These people sound very intelligent and will offer advice at the drop of a hat. What they often lack, though, is common sense. Take their advice with a grain of salt. Use your own judgment based on facts.

Those with a conflict of interest in the matter. This is someone who might be thinking, ever so lightly, about starting a cleaning business. He might want to see your business fail so that he can come along, follow in your footsteps and succeed. He might want you to fail in order to eliminate competition.

Those who caution against taking risks. I thought several years ago about buying a small neighborhood grocery store that was for sale. Those I talked to were convinced I that I would fail even though the previous owner enjoyed great success. They just could not see me succeeding in the business. Unfortunately, I listened to them and did not even try to buy the store. I later regretted the decision. Don't ever let others discourage you from starting your cleaning service business.

Chapter 4

Commercial Cleaning

Commercial cleaning refers to the cleaning of commercial facilities. These include offices, restaurants, colleges, universities, hospitals, auto dealerships and many more businesses. The need for commercial cleaning services will exist as long as there are commercial facilities. Commercial cleaning services are needed even during a recession. This segment of the cleaning industry is expected to expand with the growth of commercial real estate construction.

A cleaning business that focuses on commercial cleaning will typically perform most its duties after normal business hours when there are no customers or clients present. However, a cleaning business that cleans a hospital or an educational institution will often clean at any hours of the day or night.

Many cleaning service businesses start out cleaning small offices. This is one of the easiest kinds of facilities to clean. The work involves vacuuming, emptying trash containers, dusting, cleaning restrooms and cleaning break rooms. As your company grows, you might want to consider expanding your available services to include cleaning windows, shampooing carpets and stripping, waxing and buffing floors.

Cleaning medical offices and hospitals requires that you and any of your employees who clean there be knowledgeable in the safe handling of any equipment and waste that might contain blood borne pathogens, germs that can cause disease such as hepatitis B virus and human immunodeficiency virus (HIV).

It is your responsibility as the owner of the cleaning business to work closely with the staff of medical facilities to make sure that you and your employees use safeguards to avoid exposure.

Restaurant cleaning is another specialty that requires familiarity with health codes and requirements for cleaning. Certain cleaning products are prohibited from use in facilities that prepare food. The danger of food contamination is something that local, state and federal governments go to great lengths to avoid. You should report any evidence of vectors such as rats, roaches and mice to the management so that they can handle the problem. If you see rat or mouse droppings, don't just clean it up. Let the facilities management know about it.

The name you select for your commercial cleaning business should reflect the fact that you clean commercial properties. A name like Reno Commercial Cleaning Company does just that. Another possibility might be Acme Office Cleaning. You should choose a company name that, first of all, describes the kind of properties you clean and, secondly, is short an easy to remember.

Another consideration in selecting a company name is the possibility of your company later expanding into other areas of cleaning. In that case you might want to choose a simple name like, Bob's Cleaning Service or High Sierra Cleaning Services. Think long and hard about the name you want for your company. Take a few days to think about it at your leisure. Write down all the names that come to mind. Remind yourself that the name must mean something and that it is a name that you will view and promote with pride for years to come.

If you later decide to incorporate, you can simply add Inc. to the company name. Bob's Cleaning Service Inc. and High Sierra Cleaning Services Incorporated are examples of this.

Think, act and talk like a businessperson. Even as you start to think about start your own cleaning business, you must start the thinking, acting and talking like a businessperson. As you research the cleaning industry, you will begin to feel more comfortable looking at this undertaking as a serious endeavor. And you should. The future of your family depends on it. Money to buy a home, provide for your child's education, vacations for your family and the lifestyle that you want to live are all tied up in the success of your business. Your life depends on the success or failure of your business and how you run it. That in itself should be motivation enough for you to approach your cleaning business with all the sincerity and seriousness that it deserves.

Building confidence and determination. This business will be you very own cleaning service business. You must believe in yourself before anyone else will believe in you. Starting and running a cleaning business is not rocket science. The work is not complicated. Anyone of average intelligence or above can start and run a cleaning business.

First of all, you must remove all doubt from you mind. You can do this. You regularly clean you garage at home. You clean the interior and exterior of your car or truck. You clean your own bathroom, kitchen and bedrooms. You might not realize it, but you already have years of experience in cleaning. You are now taking the next step to becoming a small businessperson and running your own cleaning business.

Starting and running your own cleaning service business is your short-term goal. You must steel yourself and make the determination to get your supplies and equipment together and go out and secure that first account. Do not put it off. The sooner you start the better. Once you get the momentum going, you will be like a locomotive barreling down the tracks. You are unstoppable. Commit yourself to the success of your business and you will become successful. Remember who you're doing this for. It's for yourself and your family. The commitment must be firm and unwavering. Sure there will be setbacks. Sometimes you will feel that you are not making any headway. As long as you keep your goals in sight and think about them and work toward them, you are moving forward. It's alright to be frustrated and discouraged. Allow yourself to have a two minute "pity party,' shake it off and move on. There's always more study, more research and more brainstorming to do.

Your cleaning service business will always have challenges. Embrace those challenges and get excited about what you are doing. You have taken a dream and are making it reality. It's as simple as that. You are a businessperson with all the values and qualities of a professional. You know what you are doing. You are the best at what you do. That's why prospective clients seek you out. You offer a service that they need, and you are the best at what you do.

Getting commercial cleaning clients. There are surely hundreds, maybe even thousands of stores, and offices and manufacturing companies in your local area. Yes, factories need cleaning services. They need someone to clean the front office and break areas after hours. This can be you. Doctors, dentists, chiropractors, new and used automobile dealerships every other business needs to be clean regularly. The possibilities are endless. Jest sit down with pen and paper and think and write. Write down your strategy for getting supplies and equipment. Which local businesses could use your services?

Write everything down related to starting and running your cleaning business. Trust nothing to memory. Try to view every situation from the perspective of a cleaning business owner. Look for opportunities. Make your own opportunities.

Chapter 5

Residential Cleaning

You can start your cleaning business by focusing first on securing residential cleaning contracts. You will most often use word-of-mount to get customers. This is why it is important to tell your friends and relatives well before you open your business. Always have references handy when you talk to prospects. Emphasize your honesty and reliability. You want to assure potential clients that your company can do the best job at the best price.

You will often perform residential cleaning when the owner or someone else is at home. Be cordial and friendly but do not become too familiar with your customers. Avoid long conversations and gossip. Your job is to get in, clean, and leave. The home of a customer not is the place for socializing.

You will use many of the same tools and equipment to clean homes as you use to clean commercial properties. Put safety first and avoid putting yourself or your customer in dangerous situations. Many people suffer from allergies. Use only environmentally safe cleaning products. Some people find the odor of cleaning solutions to be offensive.

Equipment and supplies you will need:
- Vehicle
- Vacuum cleaner

- Wet/dry vacuum
- Carpet cleaning machine
- Ladder
- Floor stripping/buffing machine
- Rubber gloves
- Mop bucket and wringer
- Squeegee
- Wet floor warning signs
- Putty knife
- Dust pan
- Dry mop
- Extension cord
- Spray bottles
- Brooms
- Scrub brushes
- Feather dusters
- General purpose cleaning solutions
- General purpose cleaning power
- Glass cleaner
- Soap
- Wax applicator
- Hand scrubbing pads
- Stripping and buffing machine pads

You will note that these items can be use whether you focus on residential or commercial cleaning. Be sure to purchase all supplies and equipment from a reputable cleaning and janitorial supplies store.

Cleaning Techniques

You will need to give some thought to how you will clean a residence using the most efficient techniques possible. You want to get in, do the job and leave. Avoid wasted motion and unproductive activity. Get and use the proper tools. Don't waste your time and money on the latest gadgets you saw on television. Get professional quality tools such as dust pans, dusters, mops and brooms from a janitorial supply store in your area.

Pros come to clean counters, appliances furniture and floors. You cannot do this well if things are covered with clutter such as papers, toys, dirty dishes, etc. The first order of business is to survey each room as you enter. Look around to see what clutter can be disposed of immediately. When you first contract for the job, ask the homeowner about how to handle loose papers lying around the house. Most will remove their valuable papers and put them in a safe place before you start to work. If there is any question about the value of papers lying around, simply ask.

Walk around the room in a circle, clearing away trash and toys, dusting as you go. Dust window blinds, windowsills, countertops and picture frames. Make beds, dust picture frames. The technique will differ for each room you clean but the basics remain the same. Dust and clean windows before you sweep and mop.

Carry your tools with you in a tote tray. You should carry cleansers, towels, brushes and other basics.

Save time and energy by keeping your tote with you at all times.

Place your broom, mop and bucket, and vacuum cleaner next to the doorway when you enter a room. That way they will be within easy reach. It only makes extra work for yourself to have to make an extra trip downstairs to retrieve the vacuum from the living room where you left it.

You should carry a trash bag in your pocket at all times. You know you will need it sooner or later and a trash bag can be easily stuffed into your pocket.

The carry tray or tote should contain items such as the following:
- Multi-purpose, multi-surface liquid cleaner.
- Liquid degreasing cleaner.
- Non-abrasive cleaner for fiberglass tubs and sinks.
- Powered abrasive cleaner.

You might want to listen to upbeat music on you iPod or other listening device. Snappy music helps to get you moving. Listen to audio books if you are a reader.
It's a good idea to work with a partner. You can motivate each other and you can see your progress as you work.

Replenish bottles of cleaners at the end of the job. Try to think ahead to avoid running out of supplies.

When you return to your office or home, check supplies and reorder any that you need.

Chapter 6

Types of Business and Tax Entities

There are many types of business entities that you can choose to form as a cleaning business owner. It is important that you thoroughly investigate those types that appeal to you. There are certain tax advantages in starting your cleaning business under the various business entities. For this reason, it is important that you consult an attorney familiar with the type of business you want to form.

There are four major types of business entities you might consider for your cleaning business. These are sole proprietorship, partnership, "S" corporation and "C" corporation.

Sole Proprietorship

As a business owner, it is your responsibility to pay your taxes. Your tax rate and deductible expenses will be based, in part, on the type of business to form for your cleaning business. Many small operations operate as a sole proprietorship.

The sole proprietorship is a business entity that is owned by and individual and in which there is no legal distinction between the owner and the business. This means that all the responsibilities and liabilities fall on you as the owner. It also means that any profits are also yours to keep and enjoy. The owner(s) are considered the same and are legally liable and can be sued for outstanding debt of for the actions of its employees.

There are certain advantages that you can enjoy as the owner of a sole proprietorship. These include:

The owner receives all profits made by the business.
The sole proprietorship is easy to organize and record keeping is simplified.
Small amounts of money are needed to start and run the business.

As the owner of the sole proprietorship, it is you who makes the major decisions on all aspects of operations. You are the boss.

Because the owner of a sole proprietorship is legally liable for all debt, creditors are more willing to extend short-term credit to the business.

The advantages of starting a cleaning business as a sole proprietorship, there are also some disadvantages to this form of business. These include:

In many cases, the sole proprietorship is started because the owner has few resources. As such, banks are often reluctant to extend loans to this type of business. Your cleaning business will likely have to be started from personal savings and/or loans from family and friends.

A sole proprietorship has unlimited liability for your business debt. If you order cleaning supplies for your business, you are personally responsible for paying for them, even if your business closes.

In the event of the failure of your cleaning business, creditors may go to court and force the sale of the owners personal as well as business property to satisfy claims against the business.

As you consider the type of business entity that you want to start, carefully weigh both the advantages and disadvantages of starting a business as a sole proprietorship. Another type of business you might want to consider is the corporation. If you plan to start you cleaning business with family members, it might be to your advantage to start your business as a partnership or corporation of some type. While there are many types of corporations you might consider, it is a good idea to consult an attorney on this matter. You want to be on firm ground as far as taxes and profits are concerned. You need to thoroughly understand the operation of partnerships and corporations before you choose this type of business entity.

Partnership

A partnership is a business arrangement in which the parties to the partnership agree to cooperate to advance the mutual interest of all concerned partners. Few established cleaning business will be willing to form a partnership with you when you are starting your cleaning business. They have little justification in giving you the advantage of their years of experience in the business. They will also likely be unwilling to give you access to their client list. They don't know for sure that you won't end the partnership, start your own separate business and go after their clients. For these reason, a partnership probably won't be the best business entity for you. However, it is possible that the soon to be retired owner of a cleaning business might be willing to take you under their wing and help you to learn the business, later turning over the entire operation to you. Stranger things have happened. But it's a long shot that such an opportunity will present itself to you.

Corporation

A corporation is defined as an association of individuals, created by law or under authority of law, having a continuous existence independent of the existences of its members, and powers and liabilities distinct from those of its members. The word "corporation" is derived from the Latin word corpus, meaning a "body of people." In the United States, the word is generally used to refer to a large business corporation.

Advantages and Disadvantages of Forming a Corporation

There are several noteworthy advantages and disadvantages to forming a corporation. Do your homework and research each corporate form and consult with an attorney before committing.

Advantages:

<u>Separate Liabilities.</u> A corporation is a separate legal entity from its owners. That means that if your corporation is sued or if the corporation owed debt, the owners and shareholders cannot be sued or held personally responsible or liable for the action that led to the suit.

<u>Getting Investors.</u> If you intend to start a fairly large cleaning services business, it could be advantageous to form a corporation to get money to for the initial startup and operation of the business. You can create and sell shares of stock in the company and collect a large sum of capital to get our company started.

<u>Taxes.</u> Under certain corporate structures, your business can elect to have your taxes passed through and taxed at the individual tax rate. You can thereby avoid double taxation on the income your corporation earns.

<u>Gain Credibility</u>. A business with an Inc. or LLC appended to the company name sounds like a more serious and credible operation. A corporation seems to attract more clients, customers and attention from the surrounding community.

Disadvantages:

<u>Money.</u> It takes a considerable amount of money to start a corporation. Attorney fees, filing fees and

franchise taxes and over fees required by state governments can add up quickly.

Paperwork. You are required to file Articles of Incorporation in for the state(s) in which your cleaning services business will operate.
Taxes. Tax law for corporations can be quite complex. There are different tax credits and tax deductions that may apply. Thus the need for an additional attorney or account just to figure your taxes.

Under the heading of "corporation," there are two major types of corporation under which you might wish to start your cleaning business. They are the "S" corporation and the "c" corporation.

"S" Corporation.

An S corporation, for U.S. federal income tax purposes, is a corporation that makes the election to be taxed under Subchapter S of Chapter 1 of the Internal Revenue Code. What this means is that as an S corporation, your business does not pay any federal income tax. Instead, the corporation's losses or income is divided among and passed through to the shareholders. The shareholders must then report the loss or income on their individual income tax returns.

There are both advantages and disadvantages to starting your cleaning services business as an S corporation.

Advantages:

Assets are protected. With an S corporation, the personal assets of its shareholders. Creditors cannot legally pursue the assets – homes, cars, bank accounts, etc.—of the individual shareholders to satisfy debt. Unlike the sole proprietorship, the owners and shareholders of an S corporation are not legally considered the same.

Pass-through taxation. An S corporation is not required to pay federal taxes at the corporate level. Any business income or loss is "passed through" to the shareholders who then report the income or loss on their personal income tax returns. Some states apply the federal rule to taxing an S corporation; others do not. Consult an attorney.

Tax-favorable characterization of income. The shareholders in an S corporation can also be employees of the business and collect salaries as employees.

Credibility. Operating your cleaning services business as an S corporation can help a new business establish its credibility with potential clients, customers, vendors and the local community because the owners have made a commitment to their business.

Disadvantages:

Starting an S Corporation involves a considerable amount of documents, the first of which is the

Articles of Incorporation. Your S Corporation must also hold regular shareholder meetings and maintain minutes to those meetings.

An S Corporation cannot have more than 100 shareholders. This probably won't be a problem when you start your cleaning service business. You're starting out small anyway. However, later when you plan to expand your business or open new branch offices, this should be taken into consideration.

Shareholders of shares of S Corporation stock are taxed for any income the corporation earns even if they did not receive any part of that income.

S Corporations are only allowed to issue one class of stock. This restriction might discourage some investors from buying shares.

As a requirement of the Internal Revenue Service, all officers and owners of the S Corporation must be paid a reasonable salary even if the company is not yet profitable

"C" Corporation

The C Corporation is the most common kind of corporation formed in the United States. The owners of a C Corporation create a separate legal entity that helps protect their personal assets from judgments against the corporation. The C

Corporation is required to have directors, officers and shareholders.

Advantages:

<u>Limited liability for the directors, officers, employees and shareholders of the C Corporation</u>. No limit to the number of shareholders of company stock after the corporation has $10 million in assets and 500 shareholders.
<u>Unlimited potential for growth.</u> The C Corporation can grow and expand as much and as far as it chooses, including into international markets.
<u>Tax advantages</u>. Many business expenses in the C Corporation are tax deductible. Equipment purchase and lease, business travel, legal expenses and many other costs of doing business are deductible to a certain degree.
<u>Improved credibility.</u> A Corporation is view as a stable and growing business that is a leader in it industry. As such the C Corporation is viewed as a positive influence in the community.

Disadvantages:

<u>Startup costs are generally quite high</u>. Officers, directors and employees must be in place and ready to operate from the start. Most C Corporations are started by backers with deep pockets and who expect to earn a reasonable return on their investment.

<u>The C Corporation is required by law to register with the Securities Exchange Commission (SEC).</u>

This entails a whole new set of documents and attendant filing fees.

The profits of a C Corporation are double taxed—profits are taxed when they are earned and again when they are distributed as dividends. Shareholders of C Corporation stock cannot deduct any losses in the value of their holdings.

Careful consideration should be given to each of the different business entities. One of the key factors in which you choose will be your financial resources. As the prospective owner of a small Cleaning Service Business, you might consider starting out as a sole proprietorship or S Corporation. These can be started with anywhere from a few thousand dollars to a few hundred thousand dollars. It can be a family endeavor with all member of the family getting involved in the work and in the decision making process. It can be a lot of fun and it also can be quite rewarding financially.

Limited Liability Company (LLC)

A limited liability company is a flexible form of business that blends the elements of partnership and corporate structures. While the LLC is not a corporation, it does provide limited liability to its owners in most U.S jurisdictions. An LLC does not have to be created to make a profit. Professional services such as those providing medical and legal services may not form an LLC, but instead usually form what is called a Professional Limited Liability Company (PLLC).

Many businesses are started as LLCs because this form of business structure has certain tax and liability advantages over other business forms.

Advantages:

Limited liability for the owners. Owners, referred to as "members," have limited liability as an entity separate from an individual sole proprietorship. Members will not be held liable for the company's debt and other actions unless the member made a personal guarantee to back the action. If a company that is an LLC were to go bankrupt, suppliers may not sue the owners for debts owed. This means that even if the member of the LLC has enough personal money to pay for the LLC's debt, he is not legally bound to do so.

Tax feature. An LLC does not have to pay corporate tax. The company passes through the profits as well as the losses of the company. The members report profits and losses on their individual tax returns. However, the LLC may be taxed like a corporation if it prefers.

Distribution of profits. Unlike a partnership, where profit distribution is based on the percentage of ownership or investment of the partners, the LLC members may distribute profits any way they choose.

Less administrative paperwork and record keeping than a corporation.
The LLC can be formed with as many members as it wants or it can be formed with a single member only.

Because an LLC is a separate entity, its members can apply for and build credit separately from the credit of the partners.

The LLC is seen as an attractive investment by foreign investors. The LLC is a popular form of business in many countries. When investors from other parts of the world are looking for companies to invest in, they are usually familiar and comfortable with the LLC structure.
Disadvantages:

The LLC is a fairly new form of business structure. In some states, the laws and regulations are still going through transition. Some states have specific regulations relating to foreign investment in the LLC. Check with the Secretary of State for regulations for LLCs in your state.

Chapter 7

Franchise

This book is mainly focused on starting an independent Cleaning Service Business. However, you might later want to expand your business by buying into a franchise. It is always a good idea to learn as much as you can about the cleaning service industry. The information included in this section might be helpful to you at a later time.

A franchise is a business that uses another company's successful business model. A franchisor is a supplier who allows a franchisee to use the supplier's trademark to distribute the company's goods or services within a particular territory or location. The franchisor sells the rights to the franchisee and receives a fee for ongoing training, support and advertising. In terms of a Cleaning Service Business, a franchise is an offshoot of an established business operation. There are many franchise opportunities available to anyone who has the money to qualify for a cleaning business franchise.

While considering how to start your cleaning service business, it is a good idea to investigate some of the many franchise opportunities available for your area. As you perform your research, you should consider the advantages and disadvantages of buying into a franchise.

Advantages.

You will have a greater likelihood of succeeding with a franchise because it has a proven plan and formula for success. The franchise has studied the market and compiled training material that has been proven to work.

Banks and lending institutions are likely to look favorably upon an application for a loan because you are less likely to default on the loan.

A franchise has a recognized corporate image and brand awareness. Potential clients often feel more comfortable and trusting in hiring a contractor with a franchise.

A franchise company usually provides extensive training and support to their franchisees to help them succeed.

Franchises usually advertise nationally and, in doing so, they help increase sales for all franchisees.

Disadvantages.
Franchises cost lots of money to start. They also often charge ongoing royalties that cut into the profits of franchisees.

Franchisors usually require that franchisees follow their procedures to the letter. There is very little room for variation. You might not be able to express your own creativity in the operation of the franchise.

The franchisor usually expects to get a certain percentage of you income as franchisee fees.

A franchise might or might not be the best fit for your cleaning business. Careful consideration must be given to the advantages and disadvantages of having a franchise. Take into consideration your experience, assets and temperament before committing to buying into a franchise cleaning service business.

It has been my experience that a cleaning business is not like the hamburger restaurant business. Although there are cleaning franchises that will hold your hand and guide you along the path to success, I like to think for myself and make my own decisions based on experience, logic, reason and common sense. Do not be afraid of making mistakes as an independent cleaning service operator. Making mistakes is how we learn.

The average small business operation is not likely to have the initial investment to buy into a franchise operation, which can run from tens of thousands to hundreds of thousands of dollars. The focus of this book is to help you start your cleaning service business with the minimum of capital. Once you start making money, you might later consider joining a franchise, but only after you have weighed the advantages and disadvantages for an independent operation versus a franchise.

Chapter 8

The Business Plan

One of the first steps in starting your cleaning service business is to create a business plan. The business plan is the blueprint from which you will set up your business. You will use it as a roadmap that you will follow while starting and operating your cleaning service business. Your business plan will also be used to secure financing for equipment for the business startup. It can also be later used to project growth and expansion. The business plan is also used to secure initial financing from banks and other and venture capital firms for your business. Your business plan shows that you have and intimate understanding you're your cleaning services business and are confident that it will be a successful venture.

Here is an outline of the detailed information you should include in your business plan.

Executive Summary

The executive summary is perhaps the most important section of your business plan. The executive summary tells the reader where your company is in its development at the moment, where you want to take it and why you think your business will be successful. If your business is an idea that you intend to develop, make sure to state that this is a business proposal. If you are seeking financing for your business, the executive summary presents your fist chance to grab the interest of potential lenders and/or investors. Include the following points in your executive summary.

Mission Statement—The mission statement explains what your business is about. Basically, it tells what products or services you will offer. In the case of you cleaning service business, you will offer cleaning services for offices and/or residential clients.

Company Information—Include a short statement that covers when your business was started or will be started, the name(s) of the founders and their roles the number of employees and your business location(s).

Growth Highlights—Include here examples of your company's growth such as market or financial highlights. If this is a business proposal, list your best estimate of profit margins for the upcoming year and/or years. Visual aids such as charts and graphs are quite useful for this section. This section shows prospective lenders and/or investors that you have a sense of what direction in which you will aim your cleaning service business.

Graphs and chart information can be created using statistics from the U.S. Department of Commerce. There are several free chart and graph generator programs available online. Simply type "graph and chart generators" into your browser's search box.

Your Products/Services—Your business will provide cleaning services to commercial and residential clients. (As a sideline to cleaning services, you might later decide to offer air cleaning and air freshening products for your clients. Include that information here.)

Financial Information—List here information about your finances including profits, investors and banking information. Your financial information gives potential lenders and investors a sense of your company's stability. This, along with your growth highlights, can quickly signal the soundness of your business as a being worth investing in lending money or offering a loan.

Summarize Future Plans—Explain here where you would like to take your business. Look toward one year and five year projections. Every business should expect to grow and expand. Stagnation will kill off your cleaning service business. Always be on the lookout for the possibilities, wither by expanding your business to offer additional products and services or by buying out already existing cleaning service businesses.

If this business plan is a more of a proposal, be sure to list any other businesses you have managed or owned. Also show any experience you have in working for a cleaning service business. If you are just starting out, you might not have a lot of experience in cleaning services. Do not let this deter you from starting a cleaning service business. Your lack of experience as a cleaning business owner can be an advantage. It proves that you are not a know-it-all and are willing to take the risk and do your level best to succeed.

Thoroughly analyze the market for cleaning businesses in the state, county or city in which your will operate. Your familiarity with the cleaning industry will stand you in good stead with potential lenders and investors and will reinforce you confidence in your ability to run your own cleaning service business.

Company Description

This section of the business plan for your cleaning service business provides a detail overview of your business. This section can help lenders and potential investors understand the goals of your business. Include the following details in your company description.

The Nature of Your Business—This is a cleaning service business. You will also offer air freshening products to keep the clients office environment clean and smelling fresh. The client's employees will be more productive because the clean and fresh-smelling environment that you provide will help them to relax and perform at their best. Tell how your cleaning service business will fill a need in the marketplace. Explain how your initial focus will be on the office cleaning segment of the industry. Your goal is to provide the most efficient office cleaning services and the best price. You and your employees will distinguish yourself from other office cleaning businesses by being professional, efficient and willing to provide value-added service and products.

Organizations Your Business Will Serve—List the specific consumers, business and organizations and consumers that your business will serve. Her, you can explain that your will start out servicing small business offices such as doctors, lawyers and other professionals' offices. Later you will offer cleaning to retail stores and residential clients.

Your Competitive Advantage—Show what competitive advantage your cleaning service business has over other similar businesses in the area. Since you are a small operation, your business is in a position to provide a more personalized experience for clients. You are just a phone call away. There will be no wading through layers of staff and management to reach you. Tell how your operations will provide the most efficient cleaning at the best value. Tell how your business is or will be located conveniently located for quick and easy dispatch. Think about how you will be the best cleaning services business in the area. Think in glowing terms about your determination, your enthusiasm and your eagerness to be the very best.

Market Analysis

Industry Outlook and Description—Your market analysis summary should include information about your industry, its historic growth rate and present size, life cycle and growth forecast. Include information about your target market which, in our case, will be small professional offices to start. Try to narrow down your market. You are just starting out and don't want to lose focus. Contracting with ten or up to twenty small offices I your local area should keep you very busy working part-time.

Your Target Market—What sector of the population do you intend to serve? Will your business cover city, county or statewide areas? Think about the needs of your potential clients. Small professional offices need reliable and trustworthy cleaner on their property after the staff has left for the day. Your trust is of utmost importance. If you and your wife perform the cleaning duties, but if you later decide to hire employees, make sure that they are trustworthy and reliable.

What Makes Your Business Unique?—Also, think about what sets your cleaning service business out from other similar businesses. What is unique about your operations? You might mention here that you use streamlined and efficient cleaning procedures, your attention to detail and your follow-up phone call to guarantee client satisfaction. Price can be mentioned but try not to focus too much on pricing. If you are new at this business, don't emphasize your relative inexperience. Think about how you can best fill the client's needs in the area of office cleaning. You do not have to undercut other cleaning businesses in your area because you make up for it with better cleaning and forming a lasting relationship with your clients.

Size of Your Primary Market—How large is the market and what share of the market do you expect to gain in your area of operation? You might explain the construction of new office buildings in your area. Stay abreast of all new and planned construction in your area. Stay on top of things. Anticipate business development. Think of new building construction in terms of new clients. If you think you can get contracts with 5% of the new offices in a planned one-hundred office complex, state so here. Five new clients means at least five more hours of work a week for you. Always think about and plan for the growth of your cleaning service business.

How much market share can you gain?—How many cleaning businesses are in the area? Is the market saturated? What percentage of the market can you expect to capture. While there may be many cleaning business in your area, you can gain a sizeable share of the market by distinguishing your cleaning service business from the hundreds of others by focusing on professionalism and efficiency. You might not be able to afford uniforms for you and your employees starting out, but you can have t-shirts printed with your company name and the names of your employees. These can be created online by you. They can be created one at a time or you can create and buy more.

Pricing and gross margin targets—Discuss your expected gross margins and pricing structure. Also mention any discounting plan you intend to use. You might mention that you will offer a $20 discount to new clients on their first office cleaning. The idea here is to think about incentives that will get new and repeat clients.

Competitive Analysis—The competitive analysis should identify who your competition is in the cleaning business and how much of the market they control.
Evaluate your competition in terms of:

- Strengths and weaknesses
- Market share
- How important is your target market to the competition?
- What barriers might hinder you entry into the market?
- What time of year is the best time to enter the market?
- Are there secondary or less well known competitors that might impact your success in the cleaning business?
- Are there barriers to entering the market such as high investment costs, lack of quality personnel or difficulty in finding information on running the business?
- Regulatory Restrictions—Discuss here any client or government regulations that affect your cleaning service business. Tell how you

will comply. Also, cite how these regulations might impact the cost of doing business.

Organization and Management

This section of the business plan includes the organizational structure of your company, details about the ownership and the management team. Include details about who does what within the cleaning service business, their background, experience and qualifications to hold positions of management. Explain what each member of the management team is responsible for and in what capacity they will serve. Even though you might have a one- or two-person operation, it is important for any potential lenders or investors to know the roles of company leadership.

Elaborate on the pay and benefits for both management and hourly employees. Discuss any incentives you might have for employees to acquire new clients for your business. Also, discuss any promotions you plan to initiate to encourage new client sign-ups and introductory cleanings. This might seem like lots of information but its purpose is to give you a better sense of your operations. You and potential lenders and investors need reassurance that your business has structure and a team of capable managers.

Organizational Structure—Create an organizational chart with the names and departments headed by all employees. This might include owner, Supervisor of labor, Quality

Assurance Manager, Payroll Officer, Sales Manager, Salespersons and Customer Relations Officer. You might have only yourself and your wife as the total staff for your company when you are starting out. It is important, though, that each team member knows without question what his or her responsibilities are.

Ownership Information—This section should stat the details of your business and tax structure. If you are or will be a Sole Proprietorship, state so here. The same goes if you will be a Limited Liability Company (LLC) or Corporation.

Details to include here are:
- Names of owners
- Percentage ownership of each owner.
- To what degree will owner be involved in operations of the business?
- Names and profiles of management including education and training, work experience and qualifications. Also state the compensation package for each manager. In subsequent years, your will want to list any major achievements of the management team. If you or your wife increased sales by 15% of the previous year, be sure to state it here.

Service and/or Product Line

This section deals with the services and/or products you will offer to your clients. As mentioned earlier, you might want to offer air freshening products to you clients as a side business to increase profits. Emphasize the benefits that your services and/or products will provide. Keep quality in mind, both with your products and your services.

Description of Your Service and/or Product— Include here specific benefits of your services and/or products. Ask this question of yourself. How does my office cleaning service benefit professional offices like lawyers, doctors and real estate and other similar organizations?

Details About the Life Cycle of your Products and/or Services—How regularly should you clean each office. This will depend, of course, on the size and type of office. You want to try to arrange to clean each office at least two times a week to empty trash and dust and tidy up the place. Larger offices with many employees will require cleaning every business day. You can plan to check the level of your air freshening products each time you clean. After a short time, you will know how to gauge when freshening products should be refilled.

Many of these details will be learned from your experience as you continue in your cleaning service business. Don't try to fake it. If a client wants to know how often you recommend cleaning, make an educated guess. Use your judgment. Of course you want to clean each office every day, but this might not be practical for a small two or three-person office. Start your business with an attitude of honesty and integrity. Do not try to take advantage of any client. Do not try to undercut the prices of your competition. If you don't know how long it will take to clean a client's office, tell them so. This is an opportunity for you to offer them a free or reduced-price cleaning so that they can see how well you perform and you can get an idea about how long it will take. It's a win-win situation for all concerned.

Intellectual Property—Describe any trade secrets, processes that might be considered trade secrets copyrights and product you might have invented. Under this heading, include any trademark or service mark design, sign or expression that distinguishes products or services of a particular source from those of others. Trademarks are used on products associated with a particular company. If you have invented a unique air freshening product, you will want to have it trademarked and registered with the U.S. Patent Office. You can put your trade mark symbol on the packaging to identify it as being uniquely yours. A trademark is usually labeled with the symbol ® or "Reg U.S. Pat & TM Off".

Service marks are used to identify services provided by a company. Since a service is not a physical product a service mark is used instead of a trade mark. You can place your service mark on your company vehicle and in your brochures to identify your company, setting it apart from all others. Service marks are generally identified with a superscript symbol ™.

This section can also include any non-compete or nondisclosure agreements you might have with your employees. Sometimes employees decide to leave their employer and start a similar business. Here you can clarify and arrangements for just such a contingency if there are any.

Research and Development—You can discuss here any plans for future research and development within y9u cleaning business. Research into creating unique air freshening products and devices could be an area of focus for your cleaning service business. You might also consider research into the care and cleaning of the latest floor care products. New developments in the manufacture and care of carpet, tile and composite flooring is something with which you should become familiar.

Marketing and Sales

This section of your business plan deals with your marketing and sales strategy. It basically asks: How will you market your cleaning service business? You will elaborate on the means and channels you will use to advertise and promote your business to get clients and contracts. Marketing is an ongoing and continuous process. You will advertise your business with your business cards, brochures, website, direct mail sales letters, through social media and through any channel you can think of. You will also make as many connections as you can with other cleaning businesses and through many of the channels discussed in the Networking section of this book.

The Marketing Strategy explains how you will market or sell your cleaning services. A strategy is defined as: a plan, method, or series of maneuvers or stratagems for obtaining a specific goal or result. The goal is to secure clients and contracts for your cleaning service business. Your overall marketing strategy should include the following:

Your market penetration strategy—Tell how you intend to get your first clients. Starting out, you might want to focus on securing contracts with local offices of doctors, lawyers, chiropractors and similar professionals.

Your growth strategy—Tell how you plant to grow and expand further into the cleaning services industry. Always have a plan for growth and expansion. Seek other clients in other cities in your county. Later plan to expand into other counties. Your channels of distribution for your products and services—Will you hire a sales agent or will you do all the selling yourself? You will be responsible for getting business at first. As you grow, consider hiring a professional sales agent to handle securing contracts.

Communication strategy—You will use as many means of advertising your business as possible. This will include word-of-mouth, business cards, brochures, website, introductory offers and promotions, flyers and by directly approaching potential clients.

Your overall Sales Strategy explains who will handle selling your cleaning services and the means by which they will get clients. The sales strategy should include:

Your sales team strategy—State whether you are going to use a sales staff hired and trained by you company or will **you employ the services of a professional external sales** company. Tell how you will hire and train your sales team members. Discuss compensation for sales persons hired from within your company.

Sales activities—Explain here the specific activities you will use to get clients. You will first need to identify potential clients. Make a list of potential clients. Search online for doctors, lawyers, architects, veterinarians, optometrist, real estate agents and similar professionals. This is your pool of potential clients. Try to find out the name of the office manager at the business.

Start by sending a sales letter along with a brochure and your business card introducing yourself and your business. Address the sales letter to Acme Chiropractic, Office Manager. Tell them that you will call them in a few days to discuss how your cleaning service business can benefit them and their clients. Wait about a week then start calling to set up appointments.

You might have to send out lots of sales letters and make lots of calls to get your foot in the door. Do not become discouraged. You will face rejection. Just remember to use the rejections as fuel to feed you determination to succeed in your cleaning service business.

Funding Request

In this section, you will outline any need you might have for funding your business. You might or might not use this section in your business plan depending on how you intend to pay for supplies and equipment. Many one- and two-person cleaning businesses start with money from savings or with money borrowed from relatives or friends. The focus of this book is to start your cleaning service business with the smallest amount of money possible.

You might, on the other hand, wish to start with a fairly good amount of supplies and equipment so that you can provide a wide range of services. Even though you might start out cleaning only small offices, you will need a heavy duty vacuum clean and buffing/waxing machine at least. Heavy duty equipment cost more than equipment intended for home use only. It might be simpler just to get the higher quality equipment from the start than to burn out you home vacuum end up having to buy another cleaner soon after you start. Therefore, it might be a better idea to have more money from the beginning.

Try to be realistic about how much money you will need. You might be able to start out with a few hundred dollars in supplies and equipment. However, with more money, you will have more breathing room to focus on the details of running your business rather than worrying about having enough money for a computer, business cards, brochures, and other items that you will need to get sooner or later. If you need $10,000 or $50,000 state it here.

You can use your business plan to seek funding from outside sources like banks, investors and venture capitalists. It is important that you present a realistic picture of your needs before you approach any lenders or investors.

Your funding request should include the following.

- Your current funding requirement
- Any future funding requirements over the next five years
- How you will use the funds you get. Be truthful and realistic. Will the money be used for startup? Working capital and equipment? List all the planned uses for the money you will get.
- List any financial strategies that you will employ for growth and expansion in the future. Also, tell how you will repay the debt that your company acquires.

Include in this section the amount you want for now and the amount you will want in the future. You will likely need much more money for startup that you will need later. However, you just might need enough money to carry you through the first year of business operations while you get clients and become established in the local market.

Financial Projections

This section of the business plan is completed after you have the market for your cleaning services business and set clear objectives you want to achieve. Your financial projections for your business reflect the financial goals you intend to reach and along a recap of your finances if your business has been in operation for any length of time. The point here is to give lenders and investors a snapshot of the financial performance of your business. If your cleaning service business does not have a financial history, focus on your prospective financial information. All businesses want to make money. That's the idea behind starting a business. Your financial projections should include the following:

Historical Financial Data—This is an overview of the past performance of your company. Profits and losses over the past five years or more of operation should be discussed.

Prospective Financial Data and Projections—This section will be your focus if you are in the planning stages of your cleaning service business. Lenders and investors want to be assured that their money will be well spent.

Your financial expectations should extend through the next five years with monthly or quarterly projections for the first year. Each estimate should include information such as income projected income statements, balance sheets, cash flow statements and the budget for your capital expenditures.

Your projections should match the amount in your funding request. All data should match. Otherwise the lender might wonder how the money will be spent. You want to cultivate trust in your relationship with potential lenders and investors. Discrepancies in your numbers will immediately raise a red flag in the minds of lenders. Use graphs and charts to illustrate your financial projections.

Appendix

The Appendix is one part of the business plan that is optional. Lenders and investors will use the business plan to determine whether or not to lend to or invest in your business.

The following should be included in your Appendix:

- Legal documents
- Licenses and permits
- Credit history (personal and business)
- Letters of reference
- Resumes of key managers
- Detailed market studies
- Relevant book references and magazine articles

- Copies of leases
- Contracts
- Names of Lawyer, Accountant and Business Consultants

Your business plan and all its contents should have limited distribution. Limit its distribution to only those who need to know the information such as lenders and investors.

Chapter 9

Business Licenses

Licenses and Permits.

Almost every business needs some form of license or permit to operate legally. Licensing and permit requirements vary depending on the type of business, the state in which it is located and what government rules might apply.

Federally regulated industries such as alcohol, aviation and agriculture require specific federal licenses and permits. Professional such as doctors, dentists, hair dressers and veterinarians need to get professional licenses. If a business sells goods or services, it may be required to get a sales tax license or permit. Home –based businesses often need a permit from the local government to operate legally.

Tax permits. Although the Internal Revenue Service (IRS) does not license businesses, it does require that certain businesses register to receive an Employer Identification Number (EIN), also known as a federal tax identification number. The EIN is a unique nine-digit number assigned by the IRS to business entities operating in the United States of America for the purposes of identification. The EIN is the business equivalent to the Social Security number for businesses. Go online to www.irs.gov to get an EIN for your cleaning service business. The EIN is used for opening a bank account for your business and when filling out income tax forms for your business.

State, County and City Business Licenses and Permits. If you intend to operate your cleaning service business in other cities and/or counties within your state you should contact your state's Secretary of State for information on licensing.

For information on your county business licenses and application procedure, contact your County Administrator.

For any licenses that might be required by the city in which you will operate your business, contact the offices of you city hall or the offices of your City Administrator.

Sometimes the county and city in which you plan to operate your business have arrangements wherein you can get a multi-jurisdiction license.

Permits for home-based businesses. Many businesses operated out of the home get into trouble because they are operating without the necessary permits. Some states require home-based businesses to have a Home Occupation Permit. Under local zoning laws, your home-based business may not be run from your residence. You can sometimes get an additional variance or conditional use permit if you are informed by local city authorities that you cannot operate a business from your home.

The process of getting started in you cleaning business calls for planning, foresight and research. When you start your cleaning services remember this. Start small and grow slowly. You can later purchase your own supplies and equipment and charge more because you have your own equipment. Do not be afraid to ask a client if they will be supplying the supplies and equipment or if you need to provide everything for the job. In a pinch, you can rent a buffer or commercial vacuum cleaner until you can buy your own.

You want to start and operate a legal and legitimate business. Starting out, it is recommended that you register your business and secure the proper licenses and insurance or bonding to operate within your area. Since you will be a small operation to start, go to your city hall licensing division and talk to someone about getting a janitorial services business license. They should be able to provide you with all the details and requirements for starting such a business.

Before submitting the fees and paperwork for your cleaning service business, think about a name for your business. Come up with a name that easily identifies your business as a cleaning business. Something like John's Quality Janitorial or some similar name would be appropriate. After your licensing application has been accepted and approved, have business cards printed. Your business cards should include your business name, your name as owner, phone number, address, and website if you have one. A business card is necessary to project a professional image. You want to spread the word about your business and let potential clients know what you can do for them. You could also have simple fliers printed and pass them out to local businesses so that they know you can provide them with a service they need. It is very important that you constantly advertise your business with business cards, fliers or by word of mouth.

The most difficult part of starting your business will be convincing stores and companies that you can do the best job for them as the lowest cost. You will have to sell yourself, sometimes by offering introductory prices or offering a free one-time cleaning so they can see how well you perform.

As your business grows and expands, search online for standard janitorial services contract forms where you can fill in the blanks and print out hard copies. Always see yourself as a professional who is in the business of providing a needed service. Take great pride in your work and your business is guaranteed to grow, making you one of the cleaning industry leaders in your community.

Pricing your service is something that you will have to learn as you grow into your janitorial service business. Figure on paying yourself $40-$100/hour to start, depending on how involved the job might be. You might charge less for a simple sweep, mop and dust job ad more for bigger jobs that require you to sweep, vacuum, mop polish wood furniture and clean windows. This way you can cover your expenses such as licenses and insurance and make it worth your while to do the work. You also want to charge enough so that you can expand your service offerings and get a company vehicle. You also want to make enough money to purchase equipment such as vacuum cleaners and floor buffers.

A cleaning service business is one of the simplest and easiest businesses to start and operate. This business can be started with around $2,000 for start-up capital. You can become very successful in the cleaning industry with foresight, planning and lots of hard work.

Chapter 10

Bonding and Insurance

Bonding for your cleaning business is necessary in order to assure your clients that there will be remedy, in the event of loss to their property. Some things that might cause loss to a client's property are bad judgment or incompetence on the part of your employee. This might be where an employee damaged furniture or carpeting by using the wrong kind of cleaning product or by causing something to be toppled over and broken. Another case might be where an employee of your company stole some property from the client. Most office cleaning duties are usually performed after regular business hours. You and your employees are entrusted with the keys to the property so that you or they can get in and do the job.

A bond for your cleaning business can be relatively inexpensive should be viewed as a part of doing business. A bond can be secured through most commercial insurance companies. The cost of the bond can vary widely from company to company. It is generally accepted that the premiums for the bond are between .75% and 3% of the face value of the bond. The real cost of the bond depends on the risks involved and the nature of the bond. For example a bond of $5,000 might cost $150.00 per year ($5,000X .03=$150 annual premium).

Consult an insurance agent with whom you already have a relationship. This might be your auto or life insurance provider who has had experience working with bonds. He or she will be able to recommend a bond specific to your needs based on the size of your company.

You will likely have a vehicle in which you carry your supplies and equipment for your jobs. This might a small van for transporting your vacuum cleaners, mops and buckets, dusters, brooms and other equipment. You will need to have liability insurance on that vehicle since it is used in the operation of a business. Again, consult with your insurance company and your agent should be able to advise on which policy to purchase.

You need to have a bond and insurance for your cleaning services company in order to eliminate the reasons a potential client might have for not doing business with you. You your company is not bonded and insured, they have a legitimate reason to not hire you. Eliminate that possibility by getting bonded and insured before your star your cleaning services business operations.

Chapter 11

Bookkeeping and Accounting

There are several approaches you can take to keeping good financial records for your cleaning service business. You can keep your records on paper, you can use computer software or you can hire a bookkeeper and account to keep your financial records. Whichever method you use, it is important that accurate records be kept to avoid legal problems with taxes. Keeping good records is also important because your financial records can reveal whether you are making money or losing money in your business. Record keeping is a basic part of managing your business.

There are certain elements of your record-keeping that must be closely watched to judge how well your business is functioning.

Expenses and Revenue.
This comes down to what you are spending on your business compared to what money you are taking in. If you regularly spend more than you earn, you are operating at a loss. If you earn more than you spend, the difference is profit. You will always want to earn enough profit to make it worth your while to operate the business.

The simplest way to keep track of expenses and income is with a ledger in which you record credits (income) and debits (expenses). Debits are subtracted from credits to give a loss or profit. It is a good idea to keep a daily record of income and expenses. This will give you a better idea of how things are going with your cleaning service business.

Expenditures.
Keep a record of how much money your business spends. Some expenses are deductible for tax purposes. Others are not. Be sure to keep track of every item purchased with cash or by check. Also keep track of business related expenses such as computers. A good quality computer is an absolute necessity for the operation of your business. You'll use it for many things such as client lists, scheduling, inventory control and many other necessary business functions.

Accounts Receivable and Payable.
Keep a record of what you are owed and what you owe to others. It is important to pay your bills on time. It is also important to get paid so that you can pay your bills. There are software programs that make it easy to generate reminder letters to print and mail to those you owe you.

Employees.
You might later hire someone to help you do the cleaning for your clients. Accurate employee tax and income records are absolutely necessary.

After all is said and done, it is much simpler to purchase accounting software starting out. You might not make enough to justify the expense of hiring a bookkeeper and account. But keeping accurate records is a must.

Inventory.
Keep a record or cleaning supplies you keep on hand. It is usually cheaper to buy cleaning products by the case. You will not have to worry about pilferage when working alone. If your business grows and you later hire employees, it is good to have an inventory control system already in place. Another thing you will want to do is to keep a record of the serial numbers for all you vacuum cleaners and buffers.

Chapter 12

Bidding and Quoting Jobs

You will need to get clients to make money with your business. Some proposals not call for the bidding process. Others will. It is important to know how to bid a job so that you make money. There's no point in being in business if you lose money.

Quoting a price for cleaning commercial service jobs differs from that of residential service jobs. With both types of cleaning, you will include what is to be cleaned and how often it will be cleaned. Starting out, you might have to estimate the price based on how long it will take you to do either job. As you gain experience, you will get better at estimating how long the job sill take and what it involves.

As you gain more clients, you might consider buying cleaning service software with all the factors involved in doing the job. Factors such as square footage, number of restrooms, mirrors, furniture and such are entered into the program. The result is that you get a fairly accurate estimate of what to charge. This software is a necessary expense and will keep you from losing money in your cleaning service business.

Simply type "cleaning business software", "commercial cleaning software" or some similar term (with quotes) into a search engine. The quotation marks narrows down the search so you don't get a lot of extraneous listings.

Residential Cleaning Quote

There is a definite difference in quoting a price for cleaning a residence as compared to cleaning an office or other commercial business. While commercial properties may have a larger area to be cleaned, a residence often has more things to do. You might have to pick up toys and clutter in a residence while a commercial property has more open areas that have less clutter.

As an example, we will prepare a quote for cleaning a residence that has two thousand square feet of space. As a general rule, allow 1.5 hours per 1,000 square feet of space to be cleaned. In this case, we should allocate 3.0 hours to clean the home, provided nothing extra is required and it is not a home that has been neglected.

First of all, we need to determine what you will pay your cleaning person, even if you are doing the cleaning yourself. In this example, suppose you pay yourself $20.00 per hour. So $20.00 per hour X the three hours needed to clean the home equals $60.00 labor cost.

Next we need to allow for payroll taxes. FICA, state and federal taxes must be allowed for. Figure about 18% of your labor cost. ($60.00 from above) $60.00 X .18= $10.80. $60.00 +$10.80=$70.80.

Factor in supplies. A common figure for supplies is 6%. $70.80 X.06=$4.25. 70.80+$4.25=$75.05.

Figure overhead. Overhead includes administration and miscellaneous costs for the account. As a general rule this amount is 50%. $75.05 X .50 =$37.53. $75.05+$37.53=$112.58.

Allow for profit. Allow for a figure of 33% for profit. $112.58X.33=$37.15.
$112.58 + $37.15 = $149.73.
Total bid for this job will be: $149.73.

Special Note: If your state collects state tax, you must add in state taxes. Base this calculation on the state tax rate.

Cleaning Commercial Quote

When we consider what price to charge for a commercial cleaning job, we must take into account such factors and floor finish (carpeting or tile), number of restrooms, windows (some businesses have large display windows that need to be cleaned), break areas, number of trash cans to be emptied and other similar details involved in doing the job.

Measuring Devices

It is very important that you accurate calculate the area of any structure you will be cleaning. While it is possible to use a standard measuring tape, doing so makes the task cumbersome, especially if you are working alone. The solution to the problem of making accurate measurements so that you can give an accurate estimate lies in using the latest electronic measuring technology.

An electronic distance measuring tool with a laser will make the job of giving an estimate much easier. These devices allow you to measure the dimensions of the floor and calculate the square footage within the area.

Use a clipboard with sheets of graph paper attached to make rough drawing of the office area. Add up the total square footage and calculate the price to do the job.

Example. You have an office area that covers 3.000 Square feet. If you charge roughly $49 per 1,000 square feet for general cleaning, then you will charge 3,000/1,000 = 3. 3 X $49 =$147.

Estimate for this particular general cleaning job is $147.

Remember, this is a starting point for the estimate. If you have to clean break rooms and restrooms, you should charge more per 1,000 square feet since these areas require more detailed cleaning and will therefore take more time to clean than an open area.

Chapter 13

Marketing Your Cleaning Business

Marketing is defined as the management process through which goods and services move from concept to the customer. It includes the coordination of four elements called the 4 P's of marketing. For a cleaning service business this includes:

- Identification, selection and development of a service.
- Determination of the price for the service.
- Selection of a distribution channel for the service.
- The development and implementation of a promotional strategy.

What this boils down to is the services you provide and how you will promote and advertise them. There are many ways to promote you cleaning business. Some cost little; others cost lots of money. Start with a budget for you advertising and promotion. While you are considering marketing, don't forget that there are many free channels through which you can advertise such as with Twitter, Facebook, Pinterest and other social media.

Advertising is an integral part of running any business. If people don't know who you are and what you have to offer that will make their lives better, they will not seek out your services. How you will advertise yourself and your cleaning services business should be considered early on during the planning stages. There are many kinds of advertising you can use to let people know about your business, the first of which is word-of-mouth.

Tell your relatives, your friends, your acquaintances, your co-workers and just about anybody who is willing to listen. Get excited about your plans. You might come across somebody who already has experience in the field and who could offer valuable pointers on starting and running a cleaning service business. Others might know of some businesses that might have a need for your services. Don't be shy. You are a professional. You are always open to ways of getting clients and running your business.

Most of you advertising supplies can be purchased from a local print shop. They can also be designed and ordered online. Online printers often offer special deals for beginning businesses.

Business Cards. Order a supply of professional looking business cards as soon as you get your business license. Business cards are indispensable in letting people know about you and your business. Carry your business cards with you everywhere you go and give them to co-workers, friends, relatives and anybody else you can think of. They will also be important to have to give to business you contact about providing your services to them.

Stationery. Have high quality and professional looking stationery printed. Include your name, your company name, your address, phone number and website address if you have one. You will launch direct mail campaigns sending your sales letter with a business card stapled to it to local business that you want to take on as clients.

Flyers. This is another of those printing supplies that can be ordered from a local print shop or online. A flyer is a single sheet, usually printed in color that attracts attention to your business. Include all your vital information (company name, address, phone number, etc.) so potential clients can contact you. If you plan to perform maid services in your business you can hire a few neighborhood kids to take you flyers around and leave them on the front doors of homes in the neighborhoods of you city. You can also have you flyers placed on the windshields of vehicles parked in the parking lots of local grocery stores, department stores and shopping malls.

Website. Many small businesses are frightened at the thought of setting up a website for their business. They think that you need a lot of technical knowledge to even get started. Not so! Websites are easy to build and the information is available online at websites like http://wordpress.com and http://blogger.com. These sites offer free blogs (another name for websites) for free. They are many free templates available that will make setting up your blog free and easy.

Yu can use your free blog to promote your Cleaning Service Business, letting people know what kinds of cleaning services you off along with your prices and contact information. You can also offer introductory special offers and include a discount code the prospects can give you for a special discount when they sign up for cleaning services.

Radio and television commercials. Advertising on a local radio station might be something you consider later on after you have several clients. Many small businesses are frightened by the costs of radio and television advertising. They think that it will cost thousands of dollars. The cost will depend mainly on the medium. Television advertising, of course costs more than radio advertising. Some radio stations offer special deals to startup businesses that operate in the local listening area. Five short 45 second radio spots a day for a month of advertising for your cleaning service business might cost in the neighborhood of $300. It will be well worth the cost to get more clients.

Television advertising will certainly be something to consider once your business has grown to the point where you have many clients and some employees and considerable income already. Your television advertising spots will cost more because of the cost of having the television station or a video production company put the commercial together for you.

Direct mail marketing. One of the most effective ways of promoting your cleaning service business is through direct mail. A direct mail campaign involves, first of all, targeting your market. You must identify your prospective clients. If you are focused on commercial cleaning, go to the yellow page of your telephone book and find and write down the names and addresses of lawyers, doctors, hospitals and any other businesses that might need cleaning. This will be your target market. Write a professional letter introducing yourself and offer to set up an appointment so you can discuss how you can help them. Below you will find a sample direct mail sales letter you can use in your direct mail marketing campaign.

Visit Real Estate Offices. One of the easiest and best ways I have found to get clients for my cleaning service business is to work with local real estate office. The agents there know when properties come up for rent or sale and they can be an important contact when you first start your business. Property owners want their properties to be clean and presented in the best light.

The way to get real estate agents on your side is to go by and introduce yourself. Leave business cards and brochures they can pass on to clients. You can stop by the offices of agents with whom you have a relationship and surprise them with doughnuts, pretzels or bagels to show your appreciation for any referrals they might send your way. Do this maybe once a month and you will likely get more referrals than you can handle and you'll soon have to hire someone to help you handle your growing client list.

Cleaning Services Associations.
The International Sanitary Supply Association (ISSA) is a worldwide association of cleaning service and supplies companies. Its members and sponsors offer training, certification and information on the latest cleaning products and equipment. Website: www.issa.com

The International Janitorial Cleaning Services Association (IJCSA) is an international organization whose membership includes membership includes janitorial services, janitorial suppliers and general cleaning services that perform duties such as window washing, carpet cleaning and housecleaning. The organization offers training and certification in all areas of cleaning operations. The organization also offers training in the safe use of cleaning products including "green" cleaning products.

Building Service Contractors Association International (BSCAI) is an international organization that provides training and certification for owners and employees in the cleaning service industry.

Chapter 14

Networking

Networking is about meeting people. It is also about engaging people and establishing a relationship that is mutually beneficial. What this means is that you should talk to people to learn about the, their job and family. The basic line of networking is with you neighbors. It is good to know something about you neighbors. Who knows, they might work for a company that needs your cleaning services right now.

Clubs, organizations, your neighborhood watch group and just about any organization in which you participate is a good source for finding new clients. Keep an open mind and view any new relationship as being beneficial to you and to your business.

Try to become someone who makes friends easily. Do not be afraid to strike up a conversation with a stranger. Of course, you must be diligent in whom you talk to. Usually it is fairly easy to tell within the first few minutes of meeting someone whether they are willing to converse or if they don't want to be bothered.

Networking is a very important part of starting and operating your cleaning service business. Go online and look up cleaning and janitorial service associations in your area. They often have listing for contracts available for bid. Also you can network with other local members of the association to learn about new cleaning products and equipment. Always try to be open to leaning anything that can help your cleaning service business to grow.

There are many Cleaning Service Business magazines available online and in print. Your local cleaning service business association should be able to recommend a few to which you should subscribe and read regularly. These online and print magazines also have information on the latest developments in cleaning products and equipment. They often also have leads on upcoming contracts on which you can bid.

There are also several online forums and message boards where you can get lots of valuable information about starting and running your cleaning service business.

Ways to effectively network for your business.

- Attend and participate in as many local events as you can.

- Sponsor an event that brings local cleaning business owners together. This can be an informal breakfast meeting among local cleaning business owners or local business owners in general.

- Speak at local events. Offer to make a presentation about the future growth of the cleaning industry and report on the latest in cleaning technology. You can speak at your local high school career day or similar event. You can also offer to speak in front of the local Chamber of Commerce.

- Connect with other cleaning businesses in your area. Go by and talk to the owners and employees at the offices of other cleaning businesses. The owners might have some smaller accounts that are not financially practical for them to handle but they want to keep the larger accounts. The larger cleaning companies might be willing to send some business your way to help you get started. Your relationship can become mutually beneficial. The more experienced cleaning companies can also give you tips on cleaning techniques and recommend cleaning supplies and equipment you need.

- Visit local cleaning supply stores in your area. Start to purchase the cleaners and supplies you will need. Ask what solutions and equipment they would recommend. Mention that you are just starting your cleaning service business. You might even meet some other cleaning business owners while there. Strike up a conversation and introduce yourself. You are now a member of the cleaning business club. Proudly let others know that you are a player in the game. Do not be arrogant. Approach others with humility. Most people like to talk about their business and what they do. They can offer you lots of valuable information on the business.

- <u>Do volunteer work in your community</u>. You can make lots of friends and connections by simply volunteering to work at local events such as parades, city and state events such as food drives, and events to help those less fortunate. You will find that as you meet and befriend more people, they will be more willing to refer you to others who might need the services you have to offer.

- <u>Get involved with social media.</u> Google +. Facebook, Twitter and LinkedIn offer the opportunity to promote your business to your friends, acquaintances and others you know. Also connect with various communities that might need your services.

- <u>Build a website or blog.</u> A website or blog can help you get leads and clients if you do it the right way. Provide useful and specific information about cleaning. Do some research on household items that can be used for cleaning light cleaning in the home. Many do not know that distilled white vinegar kills germs and bacteria and can be used to deodorize garbage disposals.

Distilled white vinegar can also be used to eliminate mineral deposits in your coffee maker.

There are many other substances such as baking soda, lemon juice and hydrogen peroxide can be used to clean and deodorize. Write a short 500-700 word article for your website or blog about some of the many natural products that can be used between major cleanings. Make sure your website has a place for comments. Many will comment and leave an email address where you can contact them. Be discreet. Don't flood anybody's inbox with unsolicited emails. That's called spamming. Don't do it.

As you write and post more short articles to your website or blog, you will start to get readers who look forward to the free information you provide. They might not be looking for a cleaning service provider at the moment, but some of their friends in your area just might need the cleaning services that your business provides. It's all about making connections and getting leads.

Chapter 15

Direct Mail Sales Letter

The direct mail sales letter is one of the most efficient ways to get new clients. Include a pre-paid business reply envelope in the mailer to make it easy for potential clients to respond. The direct mail sales letter campaign costs little to start.

Title, First Name, Last Name
Company Name
Address1
Address2
City
State
Zip Code
Phone:
Fax:

August 4, 2015

Is your cleaning company reliable AND competitively priced?

Dear Mr. Phillip Carson,

If the answers no, then get in touch with Bob's Quality Cleaning today. With over 10 years' experience, Bob's Quality Cleaning already provides a professional cleaning service to many commercial clients in the Reno area.

You could benefit from:

- Highest quality service at competitive rates
- Fully trained and vetted staff
- In and out of office hours service
- Flexible contract terms to suit your business
- Prices guaranteed for one year

Just take a look at what some of our current customers have to say about our cleaning services:

[Get testimonials from companies you have worked for. Be sure to get their permission to use their testimonials in your advertising.]

And even if you are happy with your current cleaning company, we'd be happy to provide you with a no obligation quote to see if we can beat their price.

For more information why not take a look at our website www.websiteaddress.co.uk. Alternatively take advantage of our no obligation quotation service by calling us today on (XXX) XXX-XXXX or emailing us at Bob@ gmail.com. Please quote M-01 when you speak to us.

Kind Regards,

Signature

Bob Larson
Owner, Acme Cleaning Services

www.acmecleaningservices.com

P.S. Get 10% off your quote if you place your business with us before July 1, 2015. Just quote M-01 when you speak to us.

Chapter 16

Other Promotions

Brochures. Have full color brochures printed to advertise your business. You can include a brochure in any direct mail that you send to prospects. Printed brochures can increase your business whether you operate a large or small cleaning service business. They also serve as an interactive guide when explaining the services you offer. Because brochures are inexpensive, they provide the perfect pitch when operating on a small budget.

Postcards. Postcards are one of the effective and affordable tools to use in your direct marketing campaigns. Postcards are an easy way to share important information. Unlike many other direct mail pieces, postcards almost always get read.

Professional print and mail service. There are companies in most cities that will handle all your direct mail campaigns from printing sales letters, to providing mailing lists. They will print and mail you advertising material to your prospects, thereby simplifying you marketing campaign.

Press releases. A press release is a written statement given to the media to announce the opening of your cleaning service business and to list the kinds of services you offer. Press releases are one of the most effective ways to introduce yourself and your business to the public. You can also later issue press releases when you have special offers available for new and ongoing clients.

A press release follows certain rules of formatting and should provide information that is of use to the public. T You press release about the opening of your cleaning service business should grab the reader and hold his/her attention, prompting them to continue reading.

Parts of the Press Release.
Write an attention grabbing headline for your press release. The headline should be brief, clear and to the point. The first word of the headline should be capitalized.

The body of the press release should be written as a news story. Provide useful information to the reader without being overly promotional. Use short sentences and repetitive words and phrases. Avoid jargon and clichés. The first paragraph of two or three sentences should sum up the press release. Present the facts including the services you offer. Tell who, what, when, where, why, and how.

- Who is this press release about?
  Acme Cleaning Services

- What is the actual news?
  Acme is open for busies in this area.

- When does this event happen?

August 1, 2014.

- Where does this opening take place?
  In the greater Reno-Sparks area.

- Why is this news?
  Homeowner, renters and businesses can have more free time to focus on family and business.

Write a **boilerplate** underneath the body of the release. Include information about your cleaning service business. The title of this section should be "About Bob's Quality Cleaning".

After the title, write a paragraph or two to describe the company with 5 or 6 lines of text. This should describe your business, its policies and services. At the end of this section add a link to your website. Ex. http://bobs-quality-cleaning.com

About Bob's Quality Cleaning

Bob's Quality Cleaning started operations in 2014 with the focus of providing the highest quality cleaning services for both commercial and residential properties. The company promises to live by its commitment to protecting the environment by using only safe biodegradable cleaning products in its operations.

Print the website address as it actually is. If the press release is printed the reader simply has to enter it directly into a search box.

Add contact information.
The company's full name.
Owner's name
Owners address or P.O. Box.
Telephone and fax numbers.
Mobile phone number.
Times of availability.
Email address.
Website address.

Show the end of the press release with three # (hashtag) symbols.

###

Chapter 17

Press Release

The press release is directed at members of the news media for the purpose of announcing something newsworthy. A press release is a way to get the word out about you grand opening, promotional contest, or special offers. Your press release can be mailed, e-mailed, or faxed to editors at newspapers, magazines, radio stations and television stations.

A release made online is most often called a "news release." When distributed through print media, it is referred to as a "press release" While news releases and press releases are generally handled by the public relations department of large corporations. As the owner of your cleaning business, it is your responsibility to make sure that the public is aware that you are open for business and to let the public know what services you have to offer.

Sample Press Release

Acme Cleaning Services Announces the Opening of its New Office in the Reno-Sparks, Nevada Area

By Robert Larson
July 1, 2015

Reno, Nevada – The locally owned and operated Cleaning service business of Bob's Quality Cleaning announced today that it will open a new office in the Reno-Sparks area on August 1, 2015.

Bob's Quality Cleaning will offer a broad spectrum of cleaning serviced for residential and commercial clients. Have more free time to spend with family, friends and associates. Unclutter your life and get organized.

About Bob's Quality Cleaning

Bob's Quality Cleaning started operations in 2014 with the focus of providing the highest quality cleaning services for both commercial and residential properties. The company promises to live by its commitment to protecting the environment by using only safe biodegradable cleaning products in its operations.

Bob's Quality cleaning has a commitment to the growth and development of the economy within the Reno-Sparks area. We are a local business with a strong connection to this community.

The many services offered by Bob's Quality Cleaning include Commercial and Residential Cleaning. We offer the following specific services as requested:

- Office cleaning
- Apartment and home cleaning.
- Bathroom and kitchen cleaning.
- Floor waxing
- Window cleaning.
- Carpet cleaning.
- Floor stripping and sealing.

Contact

To learn more about Bob's Quality Cleaning, please contact:

Robert Larson, Owner
Bob's Quality Cleaning
1234 Mayfair Blvd. Ste. 8
Reno, Nevada 89501
Phone:
Office: (XXX) XXX-XXXX
Fax: (XXX) XXX-XXXX
Website: www.bob'squalitycleaning.com
Email: bob@bobsqualitycleaning.com

###

Chapter 18

Cleaning Equipment

There are certain pieces of equipment that are absolutely necessary to have and use during the operation of your cleaning service business. The first pieces of equipment you need to purchase are a vacuum cleaner and a floor buffer/waxer. You will use this equipment day after day for years so it is important that you purchase commercial quality equipment.

Vacuum Cleaner

Selecting a Commercial Vacuum Cleaner
There are many brands and types of vacuum cleaners available to use in your business. You do not want to use a residential vacuum for commercial applications. The might last for a few months and then you will have to purchase another one, costing you more money and making you lose time and maybe even a customer.

There are many vacuum cleaner distributors that sell vacuum cleaners that really are not commercial quality machines. Some distributors actually take a residential vacuum, put a three-prong plug on the end of the power cord and label it a commercial vacuum cleaner.

You will want a vacuum cleaner that is simple and easy to operate. You will likely have employees doing your cleaning and you want to simplify all tasks. A complicated vacuum cleaner will only make for confusion and loss of time. Choose a vacuum cleaner that is lightweight to make for easier cleaning with less fatigue. You should select a vacuum that has onboard tools for cleaning corners and odd-shaped sections of the floor. The vacuum cleaner you choose should also have a wide cleaning head to reduce the length of time needed to clean an area.

Make sure that you vacuum has a feature that allows you to move go from cleaning hard floors to cleaning carpeting with just the flip of a switch. The hard floor mode provides for full suction for better cleaning while the carpet mode needs less powerful suction for more thorough cleaning. A good quality commercial vacuum will also have extra-large tubing to avoid clogging.

You commercial vacuum cleaner will need to have a long, durable three-prong power cord. Try to select a vacuum with a power cord 30'-50' in length to allow you to clean large areas of carpet.

Another consideration when buying a vacuum cleaner is the air filtration system on the vacuum. Get a vacuum that has a Hepa filter to reduce the amount of dust thrown out into the air during while cleaning.

Floor Buffing and Polishing Machine

A floor buffing and polishing machine is the second most important piece of equipment you will need to purchase after you buy a commercial vacuum cleaner. There are many sizes of hard floor treatment machines available with a variety of features. The most commonly recommended size but the 20" size the most practical for your cleaning service business.

A floor buffer or rotary floor machine is a low speed machine that has a horizontally rotating head which attaches to a round scrubbing pad or floor scrubbing brush that spins in a circle in one direction. The spinning pad or brush is powered by a small motor located over the center of the machine head. Some buffers are equipped with a solution tank that can spray floor cleaning solution directly into the scrubbing pad and onto the floor. The speed at which the pad or brush rotates affects the kind of cleaning job you want to do.

The floor buffer is used to remove surface scratches and marks to create a smooth, blemish-free finish that reflects the light and gives the floor a glossy appearance. Hard surface floors such as vinyl tiles and sheeting should be polished regularly. How often you need to buff and polish the floor will depend on the composition of the flooring and the amount of traffic. You will want to polish a floor when the surface starts to look dull and there are many visible scuff marks.

Low Speed buffer. This machine operates in a side-to-side swing motion and is designed to handle scrubbing jobs when the floor has ground in dirt that you need to remove. A low speed machine is also the machine of choice when you need to strip off the old wax coating from a hard surface floor. Low speed buffers rotate at speeds of about 175 revolutions per minute (RPM).

Dual speed buffer. This machine can perform dual duty as a floor wax stripper and as a polisher. A dual speed machine operates at speeds of 175-350 RPM. The higher speed of rotation setting will result in a higher gloss finish on the floor. A dual speed buffing and polishing machine is the most versatile for use in you cleaning service business.

Floor burnisher. This machine is also known as a high speed floor buffer. It rotates at more than 10 times the speed of a conventional low speed buffer, usually between 1,500 and 3.000 RPM. The higher speed of rotation and greater weight of the burnisher results in a finish that is very glossy and has the much preferred "wet look."

Buffing and polishing hard surface floors. You will need to first clean the floor with a dust mop to remove loose dust and other debris. Install a buffing pad onto the machine. Walk in a straight at 1'- 2' per second, overlapping each pass by 2"-4". Buff the floor until the desired gloss is achieved. Work on a small area at a time. Change the pad when it becomes worn or dirty. Use a dust mop to remove the dust from the floor after you have finished buffing.

The dual speed polisher usually weighs more than the low speed buffer. The added weight exerts more downward pressure on the floor, resulting in a higher gloss finish.

Chapter 19

General Office Cleaning

Every office has at least one common area other than the restroom that is occupied and used by employees and clients or customers. Maintaining and cleaning the common areas of an office will be an important function of your cleaning services business.

Before beginning the task of cleaning the open area of the office you must assemble the tools and supplies for the job. The tools you will need include the cart, dusters, cleaning cloths and towels, plastic trash can liners, vacuum cleaner, dust mop, broom, dustpan, putty knife and spray bottle filled with water.

You will use a variety of cleaning products to perform your cleaning duties. It is important that you closely follow the directions for the use of each cleaning solution and powder. This will avoid exposing yourself and others to solutions that might cause irritation to the eyes and throat. Knowing which cleaning solution to use on different surfaces will prevent damage to desktops, computers, printers and other office equipment.

The solutions you will use to lean include glass cleaner, all-purpose cleaner, disinfectant cleaner and spot cleaner for carpets. These will usually be found in trigger spray bottles that are clearly labeled with the name or use for the solution.

Furniture polish, stainless steel polish and gum removing solution might also be needed.

Familiarize yourself with the Materials Service Data Sheets (MSDS) for the solutions you will be using. The crew leader and/or supervisor must inform all employees of the dangers of misusing each cleaning polish and solution used by the cleaning staff. All employees of the cleaning services business must know the location of the MSDS for each cleaning job.

Before starting your cleaning duties, inspect the area for any items such as torn carpeting, missing or damaged floor tiles, drapes or blinds and anything else that might be in need of repair. If an employee encounters such damage, make sure it is reported to the client to avoid needless injury to customers or company employees. The client will appreciate you giving them a heads-up on anything thigh might need to be repaired. If smoking is allowed in the office—before you dump the ash trays—be sure to check for hot or glowing embers. Do this by placing your hand, palm down, over the ash tray. If you feel the slightest degree of warmth, crush out the cigarette butts thoroughly before putting them into the trash. Wipe the ash tray with a cloth then wipe with a towel wetted with an all-purpose cleaner.

Empty all trash containers and replace liner only if it is torn or soiled. Wipe down the exterior of the trash container. Dust the tope of filing cabinets and partitions using your dusting wand. Use an all-purpose cleaner and clot to clean all non-wood surfaces. Clean wood surfaces with furniture polish and cloth. Pre-treat the cloth by spraying it with furniture polish while holding it over a trash container. This way, polish does not get onto the floor and cause someone to slip and fall.

Do not disturb any papers on top of desks or filing cabinets. Do not turn off computers or other office equipment on top of desks. However, if a coffee maker has be left on after hours, turn it off to prevent a fire hazard. Use a disinfectant cleaner to clean the mouthpiece and surfaces of all telephones. First spray the disinfectant cleaner onto a cloth, the wipe the mouthpiece and other surfaces of the telephone. Avoid accidently pressing any buttons on the telephone console.

Only use a dry duster to clean the keyboard and screens of computers. Do not use any cleaning solution on any part of the computer. Liquids can sometimes seep through seams and around keys, resulting in short circuits or other damage to sensitive internal parts.

Move through the work area in a clockwise circle. Clean glass doors, non-fabric covered walls and partitions with a clean cloth towel or paper towels and glass cleaning solution.

Clean the carpet using an upright vacuum cleaner. Use the spot removing solution for carpets as you go along. Some carpets are made of natural fibers while others are synthetic. Be sure that you know which solution to use with each type of carpet.

Use a dust mop to clean hard surfaces. Use the all-purpose cleaner and a clean cloth to clean light switch cover plates and fingerprints and smudges on hard surface walls and doors. Never spray cleaning solutions directly onto light switches as this might cause an electrical shock. Use glass cleaner or stainless steel cleaner and a clean cloth to clean the surfaces of water fountains.

The next step in the office cleaning process is to place "Wet Floor" signs where traffic enters or exits the area. Mop hard surface floors using the appropriate cleaner diluted to the proper concentration as instructed on the container label. Use cool water to mop floors. Hot water could damage the floor's finish and make the glossy surface appear dull-looking. When the floor is dry, pick up the "Wet Floor" signs and return any moved furniture to its original position.

Turn off all lights and lock the doors before leaving the office. Return the cart and supplies to the storage area and organize and replenish cleaning supplies and solutions as needed. The job you perform cleaning an office professionally and correctly is seen by the people who use the office, including employees, customers and clients. Remember, the overall appearance of the office is reflected in the job you do and ultimately reflects on you and your cleaning services company.

Chapter 20

Cleaning Commercial Restrooms

The restroom is one of the busiest areas of any commercial building. It is important to always keep this area clean to avoid the transmission of illness and disease. The cleaning of commercial restroom will be one of the most important duties as the owner of a cleaning service business.

Most commercial restrooms need to be cleaned every day. Regular maintenance of the restroom areas requires close attention to detail and a willingness to sometimes get dirty to do the job.

To clean commercial restrooms efficiently, preparation is the first step in the process. Be sure that your cleaning cart is stocked with the tools and equipment that you need to do the job. You need to make sure that your cleaning cart has the following cleaning materials.

- Cleaning cart
- Two section mop bucket
- Mop
- Handy grabber
- Toilet paper and hand towels
- Toilet scrub brush
- Disinfectant cleaning solution
- Soap
- Keys for towel and soap dispensers
- Garbage bags

- Disinfectant cleaning solutions
- Gloves
- Putty knife for removing gum
- Duster with expandable handle
- Floor scrubber for removing tough stains
- "Wet Floor" warning signs

Always start by putting on waterproof rubber gloves to prevent exposure to harmful germs and viruses that might be present. Prepare to the job by filling the disinfecting cleaning spray bottle with cleaning solution. Make sure that you follow the manufacturer's dilution instructions for all cleaning solutions. Fill the larger tub on the mop bucket with water and floor cleaning solution. Fill the smaller tub with clean water.

Remember to knock before you enter the restroom. Use a door wedge to keep the door open. To prevent damage to the cleaning cart, do not use the cart to hold open the door. Place "Wet Floor" warning signs at the entrance. Open the windows if present to let in fresh air.

Step 1. Start by removing large debris such as cigarette butts, scraps of paper and gum from the urinals using the handy grabber to avoid exposing yourself to urine soaked objects. Place urinal screens in the upright position then flush all urinals and toilets.

Spray disinfectant cleaning solution into the urinals and toilets. Give the cleaning solution time to dissolve stains while you continue with the next steps of the cleaning process.

Step 2. Refill all hand towel, toilet paper, soap and sanitary napkin dispensers. Remove and dispose of liners inside waste paper baskets or cans. Clean outside and insides of trash baskets. Make a note of any damage to fixtures, trash receptacles, trash cans, fixtures, toilet stall doors, toilets and urinals and report them to your supervisor. The supervisor will then inform the management of any needed repairs.

Step 3. Use the duster with expandable handle to remove dust from top edge of stall doors and petitions. Also dust any visible vent grills and openings. Regularly dusting in the restroom prevents the buildup of dirt, dust and grime that, over time, become very visible. Sweep the restroom floor using broom and dustpan. Use the putty knife to remove gum and any other stubborn matter buildup.

Step 4. Clean the area around the sinks by using a cleaning cloth sprayed onto the cloth. Never spray cleaning solution directly onto surfaces. Clean mirrors, wall and countertops moving from top to bottom. Clean the outside surface of all soap and paper towel dispensers. Clean the inside and rim of all sinks. Clean light switch plates, doorknobs and all other surfaces that might be touched by the hands of visitors.

Step 5. Use the toilet bowl brush to clean the insides of toilet bowls and urinals that have already been sprayed with cleaning solution. Flush and rinse the inside of toilets and urinals. Use a cleaning cloth sprayed with cleaning solution to clean the outsides of the toilet tank, walls and metal fixtures. Put the toilet seat down and clean the outside and surfaces of the toilet seat. Be sure to leave the toilet seat in the upright position.

Step 6. Continue and clean all toilets and urinals. Be sure to clean all wall surfaces and fixtures adjacent to an on urinals and toilets. Replace urinal screens as needed. Screens that contain air freshening cakes should be replaced when the air freshener is no longer present.

Step 7. Prepare to mop the restroom floor. Dip the mop into the larger section of the mop bucket that has water and cleaning solution. Mop along the edges of the floor where the wall and floor meet. Mop the floor by moving the mop head in an "S" or "figure 8" motion while working your way toward the exit door. If you are cleaning a large restroom floor, you should rinse the mop by dipping it into the clean water section of the mop bucket, the dipping it again into the larger section containing the water and cleaning solution mixture. Ring out the mop and continue the mopping process.

When you are finished, collect all the cleaning tools and return them to the cleaning cart. Close any open windows and wheel the cleaning cart out of the restroom. Remove the "Wet Floor" warning sign and return it to the cleaning cart.

Chapter 21

Cleaning Hard Surface Floors

You will encounter many different kinds of floor surfaces in your cleaning surface business. It is important that you and your crew members know which cleaning equipment and solutions to use on different floors.

Cleaning Vinyl Tile and Sheet Floors

Vinyl tile flooring is often used in high traffic areas of commercial offices because of its durability and the wide selection of colors and patterns available. This type of flooring is by far the most popular and easiest to maintain.

Vinyl tile is made up of four layers or material: 1) a urethane wear layer to resist scratches and scuffs, 2) a protective clear film layer to protect the floor against rips, tears and gouging, 3) a printed design layer that has the realistic colors and patterns, and 4) a vinyl backing layer that adds strength and durability to the tile.

Vinyl tile flooring should be vacuumed regularly using the hard floor setting on the vacuum cleaner. Do not use the beater bar feature as this could damage the flooring. You can also use a dust mop or broom to regularly clean vinyl tile and sheeting. There are many vinyl floor cleaning solutions available and cleaning and janitorial supply stores. Some of these solutions come in ready to use spray bottles; others have too be mixed with water before using. Follow the manufactures directions for the use of any tile cleaning solution.

Clean vinyl tile flooring using a sponge mop and the cleaning solution. The floor can be rinsed with clean water and a wet mop. Allow the floor to dry completely.

Do not use vinyl tile and sheet cleaning solutions on linoleum, cork, wood and laminate flooring as this could damage the flooring. Do not use soap-based cleaning solutions or mop-and-shine products because they can leave a dull film on the floor's finish. Do not use steel wool or abrasive cleaners on vinyl tile floors. Do not wax vinyl floors.

Cleaning Ceramic Tile Floors

Ceramic tile are often used for flooring in restrooms, shower stalls and break room areas of offices. They are also sometimes used on walls. Ceramic tiles come in a variety of shapes colors and styles. Two of the major benefits of ceramic tiles is in their beauty and the fact that they are easy to clean.

Ceramic tiles are made from clay silicates. These silicates are mixed then baked at very high temperatures. Ceramic tiles can be either glazed or unglazed. Glazing adds a hard outer shell to the tiles, making them better able to repel dirt and water. Glazed ceramic tiles generally have a high gloss shine that intensifies the beauty of the colors.

Ceramic tiles should be cleaned as part of the regular cleaning routine.

Ceramic tiles are held together by using what is called grout. Grout is a type of glue combined with cement, sand, acrylics and silicon. Un-lazed or unsealed tiles need to be cleaned more thoroughly and more often because they tend to collect grime and dirt more easily.

Cleaning Grout

An inexpensive and effective cleaning solution for grout can be made by mixing ¼ cup of mild dishwashing liquid to 1 gallon of water. Mix the solution thoroughly. Use a sponge to carefully scrub the stained areas of grout. Use another clean sponge to wipe away any residual cleaning solution. Dry the grout with a clean towel.

Grout in such high humidity areas as inside shower stalls will become discolored more often that on floors. Ceramic tiles tend to be a great medium for the growth of mold and mildew. Daily cleaning will prevent such growth. For darkly discolored and dirty grout and tile, us a 50/50 mix of bleach and water and scrub the grout with a sponge. Again, rinse with a clean sponge and clean water. Dry with a clean towel.

Ceramic tile floors should be swept or vacuumed regularly. Do not us any abrasive type cleaners as this will dull the ceramic tile finish and remove any sealer that is present. If you use any cleaning solution on ceramic tile floors or walls, be sure to read the label and understand the directions for mixing and using the solution.

You should regularly use a dust mop followed a damp mop to clean ceramic tile floors. Never use ammonia on ceramic tiles as this will often cause discoloration of some types of grout.

Cleaning Hardwood Floors

Many professional offices have floors that are made of hardwood. They are often installed in areas of professional offices such as law offices and in older buildings that see little traffic. When properly cared for, hardwood flooring will showcase the beauty of the natural wood finish.

The quickest and easiest way to clean hardwood floors is with a dust mop followed by a damp mop. Mop the hardwood floor using one of the neutral hardwood cleaners commercially available. Mix the solution as per the label instructions on the container and rinse with a mop dipped in clean water. Mop only hardwood floors that have been properly sealed. Mopping can cause the water to penetrate unsealed hardwood and cause the floor to warp.

Most modern hardwood floors are sealed with a surface finish of polyurethane, a sealant that is highly resistant to stains and scuffs. Some hardwood flooring is sealed using what are called penetrating seals, which are wax of oil sealing compounds that penetrate the wood and protect it from within.

You can use a polishing machine to polish hardwood floors after they have been cleaned. If the hardwood floor in an office looks dull, you might want to wax it using a hardwood wax and your floor polisher. This, of course, could be offered as an additional service to be performed at intervals between regular cleaning.

A little rubbing alcohol on a soft cotton towel can be used to remove minor stains like coffee and soda. Deeper stain can be removed with a fine grade of steel wool.

You may sometimes encounter extreme cases where the hardwood has lots of stains and spots. You might recommend that the office manager have you sand, finish and seal the hardwood flooring to add beauty and luster. A glossy hardwood floor tends to make a room appear larger and brighter. You will not necessarily need to buy a sander unless you have many clients who have hardwood floors. Hardwood floor sanders are generally available for rental at equipment rental agencies in your local area.

Laminate Flooring

Laminate flooring is a multi-layer synthetic flooring product that is made by fusing together layers. Laminate flooring is sometimes referred to as floating wood or floating stone tile because the laminate flooring sits atop a subfloor. Laminate flooring often has a design that simulates wood or stone. The base layer of the laminate is usually composed of melamine resin and fiberboard materials. The next layer is a photographic applique layer that has the design and above that is a clear protective layer.

Major advantages of using laminate flooring instead of traditional wood or stone flooring is that laminate costs less and is easier to install and maintain.

Maintaining Laminate Flooring

Laminate flooring should be cleaned daily using a dust mop to remove particles of sand and dirt. Sand and dirt tend to scratch the protective layer of laminate, especially in high traffic area.

There are many laminate floor cleaning products on the market. Follow the label instructions for mixing and using the product. Laminate floors should be cleaned once weekly with a cleaning solution to maintain the finish. Clean laminate flooring using the following procedure:

1. Sweep or vacuum the floor.
2. Use a dust mop to remove and dust particles missed by the broom or vacuum.
3. Use a clean sponge to apply cleaning solution to a small 5' X 5' area.
4. Rinse with a damp sponge mop.

5. Repeat rinsing.

Move to another area of flooring and repeat the process.

Laminate flooring does not require waxing. Applying any kind of floor wax can lead to wax buildup the leaves the floor looking dull. Regular and all-purpose cleaners are not recommended for laminate flooring as they can dull the finish. Do not use ammonia based cleaners as they can strip away the protective coating on laminate.

Basic Floor Care Procedures

Floor care is an important part of your cleaning services business. There are many kinds of floor surfaces in offices. Search the web for information on determining the composition of the floor you will be cleaning. There are certain procedures and techniques that should be used to maintain the beauty and integrity of floor surfaces. Below, you will find the basics of cleaning and care of hard surface floors.

•**Stripping** - Typically performed as little as possible due to the cost and labor intensive nature of the process. Stripping is performed to prepare the floor for a new finish when the floor will no longer hold a shine through regular maintenance. Stripping involves the complete removal of a floor finish utilizing harsh chemicals and aggressive (black or brown) stripping pads prior to applying several coats of new finish and sealer. Common equipment used are a low speed floor machine, wet/dry vacuum or automatic scrubber.

• **Spray Buffing** - A maintenance procedure to maintain a scuff free shiny finish. The janitor applies a light mist of cleaning and finish solution in front of the floor machine. Utilizing a red of tan polishing pad, this process cleans the floor, removes scuff marks, and restores shine to the surface. Common equipment used are a 175 or 350 RPM floor machine.

• **Scrubbing** - A more aggressive maintenance procedure that removes dirt, scuff marks, and a portion of the floor finish utilizing a more aggressive pad (blue) prior to applying a restorative finish. The type of pad, detergent, water temperature and speed of the machine determine how much of the old finish is removed. Common equipment used are a 175 or 350 RPM floor machine, depending on how many coats of finish need to be removed.

• **Polishing** - A non-aggressive maintenance procedure utilizing a soft brush or pad (tan or lighter) to remove soil and restore the shine to a finished floor. Common equipment used are 175 or 1,500 RPM floor machine.

• **Burnishing** - The most popular maintenance procedure. Burnishing utilizing a soft pad (tan or lighter) on a high speed floor machine to clean and polish a floor that is in good condition. This process results in a better looking floor for longer periods. This reduces costs by extending the periods between most costly scrubbing and stripping. Common equipment used is a 1,500 RPM floor machine.

• **Finishing / Refinishing** - Finishing seals fill the pours of the surface, provide a shine and protect the surface from dirt and stains. A new finish is typically applied with several thin coats.

Chapter 22

Maintaining and Cleaning Carpeted Floors

Types of Carpet

There are hundreds of kinds and colors of carpet found in commercial and residential buildings. The most common kinds of carpets are cut pile and loop pile. Loop pile means that the strands of fiber in the carpet are made of loops of fiber. In cut pile the loops are cut to form strands of fiber. There are also carpets that incorporate both cut and loop fibers.

Carpet can be made from different types of fiber. These include nylon, olefin, polyester, acrylic, wool and blends. You will encounter many different types and colors of carpeting as you go about operating your cleaning business. Most commercial offices generally use higher quality carpeting because commercial buildings generally have more traffic.

It is important that you and all your employees become familiar with the different kinds of carpet and how to properly care for them. Also, different types of carpeting have different susceptibility to staining. Carpets that have been treated with a fiber protectant are easier to maintain. Fiber protectant prevents stains and spots from penetrating the fibers. You might want to consider offering the service of applying fiber protectant to the carpets in the building. There are many spray-on protectants that can be applied after the carpet has been thoroughly cleaned.

Carpet cleaning should be a regular part of the general office cleaning process. Carpets should be vacuumed every time the office is cleaned. High traffic areas in commercial buildings will have spots and stains that should be attended to as soon as they are discovered. There are many spot removing solutions for carpeting that should be part of you inventory of cleaning products.

Beyond regular vacuuming and spot removal, carpeting needs to be deep cleaned regularly. You will have an accumulation of deep stains and grime in carpets even if you vacuum every day. Carpet should be deep cleaned at least once a month to help them last longer and to provide a clean environment for employees.

It's a good idea to visit a local carpeting supply and installation company to become familiar with the many different types of carpet. The staff will be very helpful at recommending cleaning and spotting solution for use in your cleaning business. Always keep in mind that the relationships you develop with your vendors and suppliers will go a long way in advancing your education about the cleaning business. Try to view each relationship as an opportunity to learn and to grow your business.

Chapter 23

Cleaning Tips

The following cleaning solutions can be made using simple household products you probably already own.

Simple and Easy to Make Cleaning Solutions

When you first start your cleaning service business, you might not have lots of money to invest in cleaning solutions. In a pinch, you can stretch the solutions you purchase into larger amounts.

Now you can turn your favorite bottle of all-purpose cleaner such as (409 or Fantastic)... OR... your favorite bottle of window cleaner such as (Windex) into a full gallon of super strength cleaning solution! It works great and has been in use for over 10 years in the commercial cleaning business.

All-purpose Cleaner
Combine the ingredients below (in the amounts listed) into an empty one gallon container. Now... shake briefly and then add water to the top of the container.

Ingredients and amounts:
1 qt. Rubbing Alcohol
1 cup Parson's lemon ammonia
1 teaspoon Dishwashing liquid
16oz or 1 pint Simple Green (optional)

21 oz. Brand-name all-purpose (409 or Fantastic)

Top off your one gallon container by adding water. Pour solution into a small spray bottle and your money saving all-purpose cleaner is ready to use.

Everyone likes this proven formula! The more you use, the more money you save!

Glass Cleaner
Combine the ingredients below (in the amounts listed) into an empty one gallon container. Now... shake briefly and then add water to the top of the container.

Ingredients and amounts:
1 qt. Vinegar
1 cup Parson's lemon ammonia
24 oz. Brand name glass cleaner (Windex or other brand)

Top off your one gallon container with water. Pour solution into a small spray bottle and your money saving glass cleaner is ready to use.

Chapter 24

Cleaning Windows

Cleaning the windows in the facilities involves using the right tool and the right cleaning solutions for the job. A squeegee-sponge combination window cleaning tool is best for the job. This tool has a sponge or fabric block on one side to apply the cleaning solution and a rubber squeegee on the opposite side to clear away the cleaning solution. This tool usually comes with a handle much like a mop or broom handle so you can reach higher areas of the window.

Cleaning Outside Windows. It's best to start a window cleaning project by doing the outside windows, first.
1. Gathering your cleaning bucket, squeegee-sponge tool, and ladder, depending on the height of the windows.
2. Remove screens and sliding windows for easier access to edges of glass.
3. Dust off the screens using a cloth.
4. Remove any cobwebs, dust and debris from the outside surface and corners of the window. The garden hose might make this easier to do.
5. Clean the inside frame of the window using a small brush or broom.
6. Fill the bucket with warm wand, adding a small amount of your preferred cleaning solution. Be sure to follow label direction.

7. Soak the sponge side of the cleaning tool in the cleaning solution and water.
8. Start at the upper left side of the window and make a downward s-shaped sweep until you reach the bottom right corner of the window.
9. Starting from the upper left, drag the sponge straight downward to the bottom of the window. Use a dry towel or chamois to remove excess water after each stroke. Continue across the area of the glass, making downward strokes as you go.
10. Dry the window frame with a clean cotton cloth.
11. Replace screen and any glass panels you might have removed.

Cleaning Inside Windows.

1. Prepare another bucket with warm water and cleaning solution.
2. Place a cloth towel on the floor beneath the window.
3. Use a duster or cloth to clean off the window frame.
4. Wash the window frame using the solution-soaked sponge.
5. Start in the upper left area of the wind and follow the same s-shaped sweep of the sponge followed by downward strokes of the squeegee as you did while cleaning the outside of the windows. Remember to dry the squeegee with a clean cloth or chamois after each downward stroke.
6. Dry the window frames.

7. Put away all tools and equipment.

Chapter 25

Customer Service

Always remember that your janitorial services business is *you*. It reflects who you are and what you stand for. Your character, your integrity and your temperament are all a part of who you are and can be seen in the success or failure of your business. Your clients drive your business.

One of the major problems of failure in any business is that the management and employees fail to recognize that without clients or customers, there will be no business, no income and no profits. Every aspect of your janitorial services business should be driven by the ultimate goal of 100% customer satisfaction. There is no place for complacency. An uncaring attitude will lose clients and business and income. Make every effort to instill a sense of pride in yourself and your cleaning services business.

Customer Care

Customer care is that engine that drives any business. If you fail to provide the best customer service possible, you will not last very long in business. There are certain principles upon which to build a solid foundation for good customer service.

1. The customer is the boss. It is the customer who pays you. Without customers, there

would be no sales and no paycheck for you or your employees.

2. Learn to listen. Listen to what the customer says. If necessary take notes on any problems or complaints. Know the duties the customer wants to have performed. Also, listen to any concerns or problems reported by your employees.

3. Anticipate the customer's needs. Make customers aware of all the services you can provide. Make suggestions for additional products or services such as air freshening systems.

4. Make customers feel appreciated. Thank the customers for giving you the opportunity to clean their office or home. Always project a positive attitude and smile.

5. Ask for feedback. Let the customer know that he or she can contact you by phone, fax, or email. Call the customer from time to time to see if there are any new concerns that should be addressed.

6. Treat your employees well. Let them know that you appreciate the great job they are doing. Most often, it is the employee who has the most contact with the customer. Treat your employees well, and they will treat your customers well.

7. Provide service above and beyond what is expected. Set yourself apart from other cleaning companies. You and your employees should be appropriately dressed for the job. Get uniforms or t-shirts with

company name. Provide nametags for all employees.

APPENDIX

Cleaning Service Business Startup Checklist

This checklist can be helpful as you go through the process of starting your cleaning service business. It can also be used when starting any business.

_____ 1. Write a Business Plan

_____ 2. Get Business Assistance and Training

_____ 3. Select a Business Location

_____4. Finance Your Business

_____5. Determine the Legal Structure of Your Business

_____6. Register Your Business Name. "Doing Business As" (DBA)

_____7. Get a Tax Identification Number

_____8. Register for State and Local Taxes

_____9. Obtain Business Licenses and Permits

_____10.Understand Employer Responsibilities

Resources

Here are some of the resources that will be helpful for starting and running your business.

Small Business Administration (SBA). The SBA was created in 1953. It is an independent agency of the federal government to assist, aid, counsel and protect the interest of small businesses. Its mission is also to preserve free competitive enterprise and to maintain and strengthen the overall economy of the United States of America and its territories.

Website: http://www.sba.gov

The SBA website has information in the areas of:
- Home-Based Business
- Online Business
- Self-Employment
- Environmentally- Friendly "Green" Business
- Veteran Owned Business
- Women Owned Business
- Minority Owned Business
- Business Startup and Management
- Loans and Grants for small business
- Contracting
- Education

Service Corps of Retired Executives (SCORE). This organization was previously known as Service Corps of Retired Executives. SCORE is now recognized as, SCORE, "Counselors to America's

Small Business". SCORE was founded in 1964. This is a non-profit organization that is a resource partner with the U.S. Small Business Administration (SBA). SCORE provides business mentoring services to entrepreneurs in the United States. The organization is made up of active and retired business executives who donate their time as mentors to assist new and small businesses.

SCORE provides both online and face-to-face business mentoring. The organization also offers workshops and seminars and business tools and resources for those starting and operating small businesses.
Website: http://www.score.org

The SCORE website has information in the areas of:
- Business operations
- Business finance and accounting
- Business strategy and planning
- Sales, marketing and public relations
- Technology and IT services

Forms

There are several forms that you will use regularly in you cleaning business. In this chapter, you will find some forms typically used in the cleaning service business. Make copies of these or create your own forms and keep them on file either on your computer or in a filing cabinet.

Most of these forms can be used in any kind of cleaning service business. Residential, commercial, window and carpet cleaners all use forms that contain vital information. It is important that you regularly review the client or customer information to familiarize yourself with the details and requirements of each job. Simply put, know your customer. It is by thoroughly knowing the customer that you can anticipate the future needs of each.

Other standard forms such as employment applications, invoices and billing statements can be purchased at your local stationery store or print shop.

Residential Customer Information Sheet

Name:
_____

Address:
_____

Phone:
_____

Emergency Contact:
_____

Number of bedrooms:
_____

Number of bathrooms:
_____

Number of children
_____Ages:_____

Number of pets: Types
    Indoor/Outdoor
_____

Security System?   Yes/No   Type:
    Code:
_____

Date received customer keys: Number of Keys:
_____

Additional
Information:_____

Residential Cleaning Job Proposal Bid Form

Customer Name:

_____
Address: _____
City:_____ State: _____
Home Phone: _____ Work Phone: _____
Cell Phone: _____
Cleaning Schedule: One-Time ___ Weekly ___ Bi-
Monthly ___ Monthly ___
Other:_____

Cleaning Services to Perform:

Living Room: Number of Rooms __

Est. Number of Hours: __ Pick Up Clutter: ___
Dust: ___Vacuum:___
Misc. Service: _____

Remarks:_____

Bathroom: Number of Rooms _____

Estimated Number of Hours: _____

Clean Countertops:___CleanTub/Shower:_____
Wash Sink: ___
Clean Toilet: ___Sweep / Mop: ___
Misc. Service: _____

Remarks:

_____

Kitchen: Number of Rooms _____

Estimated Number of Hours: _____

Clean Countertops: ___Wipe Cabinets: ___Clean
Stove/Oven: ___
Wash Sink: ___Sweep / Mop: ___
Misc. Service: _____

Remarks:

_____

Bedroom: Number of Rooms _____

Estimated Number of Hours: _____

Pick Up Clutter: ___ Dust: ___Vacuum: ___Wash
Sink: ___
Change Sheets: ___ Misc. Service: _____

Remarks:

_____

Total Job Hours Required _____

Charges:

Fee per Cleaning $_____

First Time Cleaning Fee $_____

Discounts / Promo Code $_____

Total = $_____

Proposal Form

Proposal submitted to: Date:

Address:

_____

_____

Job Name and Location:

_____

_____

Job Phone:

_____

We hereby submit specifications and estimates subject to all terms and conditions as set forth below.

_____

_____

We hereby propose to furnish material and labor in accordance with above specifications for the sum of $ (dollars).

_____
Note:
This proposal may be withdrawn by us if not accepted within
_____days._____

Authorized Signature:_____

Accepted: The above prices, specifications and conditions are satisfactory and are hereby accepted. You are authorized to do the work as specified. Payment will be made as outlined above.

Signature: _____

Date: _____

Signature: _____

Date: _____

Commercial Cleaning Service Bid Form

Your Company Name:
Street Address:
City, State, ZIP Code:
Phone: [(   )-   -   ]
Fax: [(   )-   -   ]

Prepared by: [Salesperson]

Account Name:
Contact Name:
Company Name:
Street Address:
[City, State, ZIP Code]
Phone [(   )-   -   ]

We Hereby Submit Estimates For The Following:

DESCRIPTION   AMOUNT

Terms and Conditions:

1. Cleaning Supplies To Perform This Service Will Be Supplied By:

_____

2. The Terms of This Agreement Will Take Place:_____Time(s)Per_____

3. Total Costs of Service Will be: $_____ and payable on ____ / ____ / _____

Quoted By:

_____

Acceptance of Proposal- The above prices and specifications are satisfactory and are hereby accepted. You are authorized to do the work as described above to do the work in a timely and professional manner. Payment will be made on the date described above.

_____
Signature of Acceptance and Date

Estimate Form

Date:
_____

Estimator:
_____

Referral: Newspaper
Yellow Pages   Other
_____

Client Name:
_____

Address:
_____

Phone:
Emergency Contact:
_____

Service requested: Daily   Weekly
Monthly   Other
_____

Days/Hours Preferred
_____

Date Service Begins:
_____

Location of Keys:
_____

Location of Fuse Boxes:
_____

Client Preferences:
_____

Carpets Vacuumed: Yes   No
        Later (Specify)
_____

Windows Cleaned: Yes   No

Later (Specify)

_____

Walls Washed: Yes
        No   Later (Specify)

_____

Floors Stripped/Waxed   Yes
        No Later (Specify)

_____

Comments:
        Tasks/Rooms/Frequency

_____

Estimated Time:
Rate

_____

Total: $ _____

Routine Cleaning Duties Checklist

(Residential Cleaning)

Duty
      Date   **Initials**

_____|_____|

<u>Bathrooms</u>

Empty Trash

_____|_____|

Clean light
fixtures_____|_____|

Clean tub/shower

_____|_____|

Clean sink

_____|_____|

Clean mirrors

_____|_____|

Clean countertops

_____|_____|

Wipe cabinets

_____|_____|

<u>Bedrooms</u>

Empty Trash

_____|_____|

Vacuum floor and beneath
bed_____|_____|

Dust blinds

Dust furniture

_____|_____|

Clean windowsills

_____|_____|

Vacuum drapes

_____|_____|

Kitchen

	Date	**Initials**
Wipe down appliances		
Clean counters		
Sweep floor		
Mop floor		
Clean sink		
General Cleaning		
Empty trash		
Clean blinds		
Wipe walls		
Dust furniture		
Polish furniture		

Remove cobwebs		
Clean blinds		
Wipe telephones		
Clean windowsills		
Clean windows		
Clean mirrors		
Sweep floors		
Mop floors		

Sample Business Plan

Executive Summary

Introduction

Acme Cleaning Services is a new cleaning service specializing in office cleaning and serving the Reno-Sparks, Nevada area. The business will sell office cleaning and related services to businesses with office spaces of any size. To that end, Acme Cleaning Services seeks funding for equipment and initial operations of the business.

The Company

Established in 2014, Acme Cleaning Services offers office cleaning, floor treatment, carpet cleaning, and window cleaning for businesses with office space in the Reno-sparks, Nevada area. The business was founded by John Doe and Jane Doe, cleaning industry professionals with decades of collective experience, who have pooled their resources to develop a strategy for reaching and serving business clients. The business will operate out of a central office and storage facility and use the labor of trained cleaning crews to serve clients.

Services

Services offered will be based around basic office cleaning scheduled on a monthly basis, which will be offered with the utmost care for the client's privacy, security, and assets. Additional services will be sold to the same clients to deepen their relationship with Acme Cleaning Services. Organizational services will be introduced after three years. Services will be environmentally friendly, both in the products used and in our methods of their disposal.

The Market

The market currently consists of 40,000 small, medium, and large office businesses. Healthy growth is expected for this market, especially for small offices which will be the initial target market for the business. Focusing on small offices will establish the reputation of the company by working with a variety of clients and will force the streamlining of operations.

Financial Results

The business expects to reach $1 million in annual sales in its second year of operation and begin to pay dividends to investing partners in its first year. Net profit of $70,000 will be achieved in the first year and will double in the second year. Break-even will be achieved quickly, partially due to the fact that the management is experienced with sales, marketing, and operations, and that all cleaning crews will be paid only for hours worked, reducing the payroll risk for the business.

Objectives

Acme Cleaning Services seeks to establish itself as a leader in office cleaning in the Reno-Sparks, Nevada area. Specific objectives we will seek to meet over the next two years include:

•To build a substantial, regular client base of 100 clients on monthly cleaning plans, for a total of over 800,000 square feet of office cleaning each month.
•To build operations infrastructure, including a central headquarters, 5 delivery vans, professional management, and documented processes for operations and cleaning practices.
•To build healthy gross margins by establishing itself as a significant buyer and reducing vendor pricing on cleaning supplies and by training low-cost labor to be more productive.
•To create a culture of productivity and resourcefulness for all staff by encouraging the best ideas and cleaning procedures to rise to the top and rewarding cleaning crew for their contributions.

Mission

Acme Cleaning Services seeks to ensure that businesses have a clean office environment to support the work they do and forget their worries about office cleaning. The company values its employees to clean well and clean smart, listens to the needs of its client to do the job they need done, and responds to the demands of the environment.

Keys to Success

To become successful in the office cleaning business, Acme Cleaning Services must:
•Foster an environment of employee empowerment from day one of operation to make sure cleaning crews clean well (thoroughly and carefully) while cleaning smart (efficiently)
•Listen attentively to the needs of the client and communicate this information effectively to cleaning crews
•Research and remain experts in knowledge of the greenest cleaning practices and products
•Remember that the cleaning must meet or exceed client expectations to be considered done

Company Summary

Acme Cleaning Services is an office cleaning business located in Reno, Nevada. Established in 2014, the business offers office cleaning, floor treatment, carpet cleaning, and window cleaning for businesses with office space in the Reno-Sparks, Nevada area. The business was founded by John Doe and Jane Doe, cleaning industry professionals with decades of collective experience, who have pooled their resources to develop a new strategy for reaching and serving business clients.

Company Ownership

Acme Cleaning Services is an S Corporation currently owned 51% by John Doe and 49% by Jane Doe, the founders and directors of the company. Once additional investment has been contributed by angel investors, those investors will own 49% of the business, John Doe will own 26% and Jane Doe will own 25%.

Start-up Summary

The startup expenses for the business reflect the legal permitting required in the state of Nevada, the legal agreements with additional investors and banks for financing, two month's security deposit at an estimated $2,500 per month and one month's rent for improvements to the office and storage facility, improvements including lighting fixtures, storage cabinets, and sinks, and office supplies and computer supplies for three workstations (two founders and one administrator).

Assets which must be purchased include office furniture and computers for the office, cleaning equipment including buffing machines, vacuums, and basic tools (mops, brooms, buckets, etc.), and one service van.

Some of the larger pieces equipment can be purchased with seller-financing, such as the delivery van and buffing machines. Otherwise, it is most economical or required to pay for these expenses and assets in cash.

Start-up Requirements
Start-up Expenses
Legal
$2,000

Stationery
$2,000 Insurance
$3,000
Rent
$7,500
Computer Systems
$5,000
Office Supplies
$2,000
Facility Leasehold Improvements
$10,000
Other
$2,000
Total Start-up Expenses
$33,500

Start-up Assets
Cash Required
$60,000
Other Current Assets
$5,000
Long-term Assets
$40,000
Total Assets
$105,000
Total Requirements
$138,500

Services

Services to be offered by Acme Cleaning Services
will focus specifically on office spaces and include:

•Office cleaning (including garbage removal, dusting and cleaning of all surfaces,   sweeping and mopping of floors, and cleaning of doors and walls as needed)
•Furniture cleaning
•Floor waxing
•Floor stripping and sealing
•Carpet cleaning
•Window cleaning
•Bathroom and kitchen area cleaning

In the future, Clean Office Pros will provide office organization and de-cluttering services through an interior designer. This service will be provided as an upsell to this foundation of services.

Market Analysis Summary

The market for office cleaning in the Reno-Sparks area includes small offices (1-5 employees), medium offices (6-20 employees) and large offices (21 employees and up). In the Reno-Sparks area, businesses with offices are growing as the service sector increases, with a net of 3,000 new businesses established in 2013. Due to the economic renewal occurring in this community, this growth is expected to continue over the next two years. Small offices are targeted as well as large, although margins will be lower due to the increased amount spent on sales and travel relative to medium and large offices, because many small businesses will expand, giving Acme Cleaning Services a foothold in this market by the time competitors are willing to sell to them.

Market Segmentation

The market for Acme Cleaning Service is comprised of small offices, medium offices and large offices in the Reno-Sparks, Nevada area.

Small Offices: Either newly established ventures, or small businesses designed to remain small, few cleaning businesses seek to serve this market because of the cost in doing so. Therefore, business owners generally require employees to do their own cleaning, assuming they are saving money through this work. Acme Cleaning Services must show these businesses not only that they do not save money by having employees do this work, but that by having professional cleaners maintain their offices they will increase morale, productivity, and their appearance to customers, if customers/clients enter their office spaces.

Medium Offices: This group has a growing acceptance of the need for professional cleaning services and is concerned primarily about price.

Large Offices: This group accepts the need to outsource their office cleaning to professionals and is interested in working with vendors who can handle specific requests and take care to protect the information, security, and equipment within their office spaces.

Market Analysis

The market analysis forecasts give a breakdown of the kinds and sized of offices or residences in your area. Include here any charts and graphs that show the distribution of cleaning business contracts by size.

Target Market Segment Strategy

Acme Cleaning Services will build its expertise from the ground up, by building a successful base of small-office clients, moving on to medium-office clients and then large-office clients. While larger clients will not be turned away as the business starts out, it is expected that they will be more likely to use Acme Cleaning Services after its record of customer service and operational success is established by work with numerous smaller clients. Furthermore, by working with smaller clients first, the business will establish a foothold faster as they will not be competing directly with established cleaning companies, and will be able to work towards making this organization more profitable through economies of scale and tight operations.

Acme Cleaning Services will not work for landlords, providing building janitorial services. Many firms specialize in this service already, and marketing janitorial services to buildings involves different promotional activities, operations, and cleaning skills, to a certain extent. By specializing in commercial office cleaning, Acme Cleaning

Services will increase its ability to market to the many thousands of area businesses directly.

Service Business Analysis

The office cleaning industry includes many local companies as well as some national franchises. Services are purchased directly by business managers and owners for small businesses and by purchasing agents, office managers, and procurement specialists for larger businesses. Businesses desire ongoing relationships with cleaning vendors where they do not have to worry about the cleaning process, but will be concerned if they are paying higher than market rates. Businesses appreciate the ability of a company to quote monthly cleaning rates to make costs less variable, but also to handle special cleaning request as they arise. Cleaning vendors are sought out through internet searches, the yellow pages, and business referrals.

Financial analysts report that the commercial cleaning industry is recession resistant and highly stable. Commercial cleaning overall was an $100 billion industry in 2013 and is one of the fastest growing industries in the US, with projected growth to $150 billion per year by 2014

Competition and Buying Patterns

The commercial cleaning industry is very fragmented with no one company owning more than 6% of the market. Franchises account for 10%

of the market and local companies account for 90%. Top franchises include White Lotus Inc., ServiceMaster Clean, Reno Office Cleaning, Super Clean Janitorial, and Hanks Cleaning Services.

Customers seek out cleaning services based on a combination of reputation, price, and depth of services offered. While large offices value depth of services more so, smaller firms put a greater value on price.

Strategy and Implementation Summary

Acme Cleaning Services has selected the following priorities for its rollout strategy:

•To begin by targeting small offices to gain a foothold in the Reno-Sparks, Nevada office cleaning market.
•To leverage the reputation and experience from work with small offices to increasingly seek medium and large office clients in the third year of operation.
•To rapidly scale up organizational infrastructure, including cleaning crews, equipment, and vans.

Competitive Edge

Acme Cleaning Services will develop a competitive edge based on its utilization of the skills, ideas, and productivity of its employees. By encouraging and rewarding employee initiative and ingenuity to discover the best ways to clean well and smart, morale will be increased, making Acme Cleaning

Services a more desirable place to work. The reputation of the firm as a great place to work will increase application rates and the strength of new hires, reducing the costs of turnover and training. Customer satisfaction will increase and costs will drop due to this focus on employee utilization.

Initial training by John Doe and Jane Doe will be for cleaning crew heads. This will be ten hours of training in Acme Cleaning Services methods for experienced cleaning personnel. Cleaning crew heads will each provide ten hours of training, in turn, for new members of their cleaning crews when they are brought in to the business, based both on Acme Cleaning Services methods and basic cleaning skills (depending on the current skills of the crew member).

All client information about the cleaning will be transferred to a detailed job sheet which will be discussed with the cleaning crew head before reaching the job site. The cleaning crew head will go through a tour and inspection of the job site while the client is present to insure that the job sheet is complete and that all information about keys, security, and access is understood. Cleanings will always be run by a cleaning crew head and a crew of one to four members. After the crew have experience on a site, a cleaning crew head may move between a few job sites to supervise a greater number of jobs over one day.

Marketing Strategy

The marketing strategy for Acme Cleaning Services begins with its initial target market of small offices.

Promotional activities in the startup phase will include:

•Local Trade Show Booths at Office Services and Entrepreneurial trade shows
•Blogging, Newsletters, and Microblogging to establish Acme Cleaning Services as the leaders in office cleaning
•Prospecting by phone to cold and warm leads
•Business networking to generate qualified leads
•Coupons for free trials for new businesses passed on through the local Small Business Development Center and Chamber of Commerce

From the startup period onward, the following promotional activities will be important:

•Search engine marketing through text ads around office cleaning keywords in the local area
•Search engine optimization to improve organic search rankings
•Yellow page listing
•Local TV commercials

These ongoing promotional activities are reflected as marketing expenses on the Acme Cleaning Services Profit and Loss statement.

Sales Strategy

Sales will be managed by co-founder John Doe. John Doe expects about ten small business clients from his previous work at JAN-PRO to move to Acme Cleaning Services upon learning of their value proposition. This will account for a starting base of clients for the business.

The sales process will begin with a short phone conversation to go over the basics of the services offered and to qualify the customer as one interested in regular cleanings. An in-person meeting at the customer's office will follow, after which a proposal for a monthly rate for cleaning will be given. A follow up with the client will occur after the first three regular cleanings to get additional feedback and to continue to adjust the directions to the cleaning crew.

Before inquiries begin to come in through advertising, John Doe will prospect for sales through business networking, cold calls, and warm calls. Acme Cleaning Services expects 5% of cold calls, 20% of warm calls, and 30% of networking leads to yield regular customers.

As a partner in the business, John Doe will be compensated through a base salary, dividends and appreciation of the company's stock. After two years of operation, an additional salaried salesperson will be hired who will be compensated for sales through quarterly bonuses and John Doe will remain sales manager.

Sales Forecast

Growth is expected to speed up rapidly over the first two years as small-office customers are sought out and sold to. After the first two years growth will slow as operations must be continually increased to allow for greater growth. However, the additional target market of medium and large offices will be accessed starting in the third year of operation. Sales will be driven by the basic office cleaning service. Based on the previous success of John Doe as a seller of commercial cleaning, these projections are reasonable, as John Doe sold $3 million in cleaning services in his last full year at JAN-PRO. The additional services will be sold as add-ons to clients who purchase office cleaning. It is estimated that 50% of clients will purchase some additional services.

The forecast is also supported by the fact that, after the first year of operations, medium offices will be targeted as well, increasing the rate of growth as each sale will bring a higher square footage of space to clean.

Direct costs include the labor of cleaning crew members and the cleaning crew head, cleaning supplies and gasoline or other transit costs for crew and equipment. Cleaning Crew Head supervision of jobs is expected to cost 5% of sales and Cleaning Crew (Hourly) wages for the execution of cleanings is expected to cost 27.5% of sales.

To ensure that sales are profitable, John Doe will not be compensated on commission by sales, but by profits, after a reasonable base salary. This will keep gross margins around the industry average of 68%.

Sales Monthly

Include here your sales projections for at least six months. Show charts, graphs and any other visual displays to better portray your anticipated sales growth.

Sales by Year

Include here any graphics to show projected sale for the next 3-5 years.

Milestones

John Doe will head the sales activities, including prospecting and networking to generate leads. Jane Doe will manage the marketing and promotional activities including two trade shows (in January and February), the TV ad production (through a video production vendor), initial search engine optimization (through an SEO vendor), and the coupon campaign, which will cover three months of basic office cleaning for small-office clients.

Cover Page

INSTRUCTIONS: The Cover Page should include the following: plan name, company name, company address, company phone and fax, an email address and possibly a revision number or copy number.

Type your Cover Page text here.

Legal Page

Confidentiality Agreement

The undersigned reader acknowledges that the information provided by _____ in this business plan is confidential; therefore, reader agrees not to disclose it without the express written permission of _____.
It is acknowledged by reader that information to be furnished in this business plan is in all respects confidential in nature, other than information which is in the public domain through other means and that any disclosure or use of same by reader, may cause serious harm or damage to

_____.
Upon request, this document is to be immediately returned to _____.

_____
Signature

_____
Name (typed or printed)

_____
Date

This is a business plan. It does not imply an offering of securities.

Table of Contents

7.0 Financial Plan

7.1 Start-up Funding
a. Table: Start-up Funding

7.2 Projected Profit and Loss
a. Table: Profit and Loss

(Business Plan Blank Template)

1.0 Executive Summary

INSTRUCTIONS: Summarize the key points of your business plan.

2.0 Company Summary

INSTRUCTIONS: Describe your company, who you are, where you operate.

2.1 Start-up Summary

INSTRUCTIONS: Summarize your Start-up table numbers, both expenses and assets.

Table: Start-up Requirements

Start-up Expenses
Expense 1 $?
Expense 2

$?
Expense 3 $?
Expense 4 $?
Expense 5 $?
Expense 6 $?
Total Start-up Expenses **$?**

Start-up Assets
Cash Assets $?
Other Current Assets $?
Long-term Assets $?
Total Assets **$?**
Total Requirements **$?**

3.0 Services

INSTRUCTIONS: Describe the products and/or services you offer, how they are provided and by whom, and plans for future service offerings.

4.0 Market Analysis Summary

INSTRUCTIONS: Describe the different groups of target customers included in your market analysis and explain why you are selecting these as targets. Enter your topic text here.

Table: Market Analysis

	Year 1	Year 2	Year 3
Potential Cust. Growth			
Segment 1 Services	? % $?	$?	$?
Segment 2 Products $?	? % $?	$?	$?
Segment 3 Misc. Prod $?	? % $?	$?	$?
Total $	? % $?	$?	$?

5.0 Strategy and Implementation Summary

INSTRUCTIONS: Summarize the organizational strategy for target marketing, sales and marketing activities, and product/service development. Build a focused, consistent sales and marketing strategy.

Type your topic text here.

5.1 Sales Forecast

INSTRUCTIONS: Use this section to explain the Sales Forecast Table

Table: Sales Forecast

Sales	Year 1	Year 2	Year 3
Row 1	$0	$0	$0
Row 2	$0	$0	$0
Row 3	$0	$0	$0
Total Sales	$0	$0	$0

Direct Cost of Sales	Year 1	Year 2	Year 3
Row 1	$0	$0	$0
Row 2	$0	$0	$0
Row 3	$0	$0	$0
Subtotal Direct Cost of Sales	$0	$0	$0

INSTRUCTIONS: Use this topic to explain the Sales Forecast table.
Type your topic text here.

Milestones
Include major goals, dates and staff responsible for achieving the goals.

6.0 Management Summary

INSTRUCTIONS: Describe the management and personnel structure of the company, including any gaps that need to be filled.
Enter your topic text here.

7.0 Financial Plan

INSTRUCTIONS: Summarize the financial aspects of your business plan.
Enter your topic text here.

7.1 Start-up Funding

INSTRUCTIONS: Explain where your funding will come from, in what form (as investments and/or loans), and how this funding will cover the start-up requirements outlined in the Start-up table.

Type your topic text here.

Table: Start-up Funding
Start-up Expenses to Fund
    $?
Start-up Assets to Fund
    $?
Total Funding Required
    $?

Assets
Non-cash Assets from Start-up
    $?

Cash Requirements from Start-up
$?
Additional Cash Raised
$?
Cash Balance on Starting Date
$?
Total Assets
$?

Liabilities and Capital

<u>Liabilities</u>
Current Borrowing
$?
Long-term Liabilities
$?
Accounts Payable (Outstanding Bills)
$?
Other Current Liabilities (interest-free)
$?
Total Liabilities
$?

<u>Capital</u>

Planned Investment
Owner
$?
Investor
$?
Additional Investment Requirement
$?
Total Planned Investment
$?
Loss at Start-up (Start-up Expenses)
$0

Total Capital
$?

Total Capital and Liabilities
$?

Total Funding
$?

7.2 Projected Profit and Loss

INSTRUCTIONS: Explain the important points of your Profit and Loss projections, such as percentage increase in sales and profits, your gross margins, and key budget items.
Type your topic text here.

Table: Profit and Loss

	Year 1	Year 2	Year 3
Sales	$?	$?	$?
Direct Cost of Sales	$?	$?	$?
Other Costs of Sales	$?	$?	$?
Total Cost of Sales	$?	$?	$?
Gross Margin	$?	$?	$?
Gross Margin %	$? %	? %	? %
Expenses			
Expense 1	$?	$?	$?
Expense 2	$?	$?	$?
Depreciation	$?	$?	$?
Rent	$?	$?	$?
Utilities	$?	$?	$?
Insurance	$?	$?	$?
Payroll Taxes	$?	$?	$?

Other	$?	$?	$?
Total Operating Costs	**$?**	**$?**	**$?**

Profit Before Interest & Taxes

		$?	$?
	$?		
EBITDA		$?	$?
$?			
Interest Expense		$?	$?
$?			
Taxes Incurred		$?	$?
$?			
Net Profit		**$?**	**$?**
$?			
Net Profit/Sales		**?%**	**?%**

A Final Note

We hope that the content provided her will act as a guide and encouragement for you to start and run your own commercial or residential cleaning business. When you take up the challenge, keep in mind that starting a commercial or residential cleaning business is not "rocket science." It has been done many times before and it will be done many times in the future. The point is that you take immediate steps to start your business and reap the rewards of making your own decisions and enjoy the financial benefits of being an independent small business owner.

www.ingramcontent.com/pod-product-compliance
Lightning Source LLC
Chambersburg PA
CBHW051651170526
45167CB00001B/419